đây/đó (here/there)

Craft for Social Change series

Series editor: Hinda Mandell

The Craft for Social Change series spotlights original scholarship about how craft objects are created and deployed to enact social reform and express dissent to the reigning political order and social status quo. The series generously defines and enthusiastically embraces a big-tent approach to craft by medium, historical era, technical approach, level of expertise, and geographic location of the craftwork. The series welcomes submissions from interested scholars, curators, makers, and activists.

đây/đó
(here/there)

Cross-Cultural Craft and Design Exchange

Grace McQuilten
Rimi Khan
Becky Lu
Nguyễn Ngọc Thảo
Tammy Wong Hulbert

With contributions from
Nguyễn Thị Thu Hà
Vũ Thảo
Dewi Cooke
Jennifer Conroy-Smith

RIT Press
Rochester, New York

Copyright © 2026 Rochester Institute of Technology, Grace McQuilten, Rimi Khan, Becky Lu, Nguyễn Ngọc Thảo, Tammy Wong Hulbert, Nguyễn Thị Thu Hà, Vũ Thảo, Dewi Cooke, and Jennifer Conroy-Smith

No part of this book may be reproduced in any form or by any mechanical or electronic means without permission of the publisher and/or the copyright holders, except in the case of brief quotations.

Published and distributed by:
RIT Press
90 Lomb Memorial Drive
Rochester, New York 14623
https://press.rit.edu

Printed in the United States of America

ISBN 978-1-956313-32-1 (print)
ISBN 978-1-956313-33-8 (electronic)

Library of Congress Control Number: 2026935001

Cover: Digital illustration based on Figure 2.7.
See page 36 for original image.
Designed by Marnie Soom

We gather on the traditional territory of the Onöndowa'ga:' or "the people of the Great Hill." In English, they are known as Seneca people, "the keeper of the western door." They are one of the six nations that make up the sovereign Haudenosaunee Confederacy.

We honor the land on which RIT was built and recognize the unique relationship that the Indigenous stewards have with this land. That relationship is the core of their traditions, cultures, and histories. We recognize the history of genocide, colonization, and assimilation of Indigenous people that took place on this land. Mindful of these histories, we work towards understanding, acknowledging, and ultimately reconciliation.

The authors wish to acknowledge the Traditional Custodians of the lands on which this work was created. From Naarm/Melbourne, we acknowledge the Woi wurrung and Boon wurrung language groups of the eastern Kulin Nation on whose unceded lands much of the research, writing, and editing of this book took place. We pay our respects to their ancestors and elders past and present and recognize their continuing connection to country, culture and community.

From Vietnam, we acknowledge the Indigenous peoples and local communities whose ancestral lands and cultural heritage have shaped the environments and practices explored in this book. We honor the many ethnic groups who have stewarded these landscapes for generations. We are grateful for the opportunity to work on these lands and commit to learning from and supporting custodians of country and community as we pursue more just and sustainable futures.

Contents

Illustrations

CHAPTER ONE

đây/đó (here/there): Cross-Cultural Craft and Design Exchange

What is the potential for transnational collaboration to support the exchange of craft knowledge, cultural heritage, sustainability practices (including the cultural, social, economic, and environmental facets of sustainability), and professional development for craft and design practitioners in the Asia Pacific? As we will argue in this book, cross-cultural collaboration has an important role to play in supporting the long-term vitality of craft practices that connect cultural histories; challenge hierarchies of value in art, craft, and design worlds; and provide sustainable sources of income in addition to contributing to environmental sustainability in a time of ecological crisis. This chapter will explore some of these issues while setting the scene for the following chapters. Throughout this book we will consider innovative practices across fashion, textiles, ceramics, and furniture making in Vietnam and Australia that connect with cultural traditions—acknowledging that the idea of tradition is complex and multifaceted, as we will see in the creative practices of artists, craftspeople, and designers in this book—and foreground sustainability. We will consider the role of craft in times of crisis and reflect on the opportunities and challenges of cross-cultural ways of working toward sustainability goals.

As a coauthoring and collaborative team, we bring together multiple positionalities. Rimi Khan is a Bangladeshi Australian researcher whose work examines diversity and sustainability politics in the creative industries and who has lived and worked in Saigon, Singapore, and Naarm/Melbourne.[1] Grace McQuilten is an art historian and curator of Anglo descent based in Naarm/Melbourne,[2] with familial connections to Vietnam via her Vietnamese Australian partner and children. Becky Lu is a British Vietnamese Chinese multidisciplinary artist currently based in Saigon. Nguyễn Ngọc Thảo is a Vietnamese Australian artist and educator, practicing in Naarm/Melbourne. Tammy Wong Hulbert is a Chinese Australian artist, curator, and lecturer of arts management, also based in Naarm/Melbourne. The title of this book, *đây/đó (here/there)*, reflects our shared interests in cross-cultural learning that challenges dominant hierarchies, particularly through emphasizing the value of an Asia Pacific perspective in contemporary craft discourse and celebrating the vital role of craft in shaping understandings of sustainability in contemporary art and design.

Our approach builds on the significant work of scholars addressing the colonial histories of Europe and the United States, thinking through strategies for decentering these dominant cultural forces and decolonizing research through praxis. As Catherine Walsh and Walter Mignolo argue in their book *On Decoloniality*, this is a complex process of "creating and illuminating pluriversal and interversal paths that disturb the totality from which the universal and the global are most often perceived" (Mignolo and Walsh 2018, 2). We aim to contribute to this task by emphasizing the voices of researchers and creatives in Vietnam and Australia, highlighting the contributions of the Asian Pacific region to art, craft, and design knowledge.

The research stems from a deeply collaborative and long-term craft and design exchange project, *đây/đó (here/there)*, with creatives in Naarm/Melbourne, Australia, and creatives in Hanoi, Saigon, and Sa Pa, Vietnam. The heart of this project is a series of cross-cultural mentorships that have inspired collaboration and reciprocal learning. There is a reason that our collaboration with creatives from Australia and Vietnam evolved through the lens of "mentorship"—an approach that could be seen to privilege an unequal partnership. The focus on mentorship was a direct response to a call to action from cultural leadership in Vietnam, including Dr. Nguyễn Thị Thu Hà at the Vietnam National Institute of Culture and Arts Studies (VICAS) and the organizers of Vietnam Design Week, to provide international professional development opportunities for emerging creative talent. In the context of these efforts at "development" and "exchange," which have lots of positive benefits for Vietnamese practitioners, we acknowledge that there is an ongoing challenge of supporting and foregrounding local cultural autonomy. We have grappled with this challenge through the lens of "cultural complexity," an idea that describes the dynamic, interdependent networks that structure human and nonhuman relationships (Ang 2011), leading to the ongoing adaptation and renewal of human societies (Duxbury and Jeannotte 2011). It is this emphasis on interdependence that shapes our approach to cross-cultural encounter and exchange. Meaningful exchange, rather than systems that reinforce hierarchical relationships, involves ongoing cultural labor, negotiation, and relationship building between institutional stakeholders and creatives in different places. This relationality of cross-cultural work and the "sociality of decolonisation" (Khan 2023) emerge through our practical efforts at collaboration, mentorship, and reciprocity throughout the project.

The background to this book is the value of important histories of craft practices that intersect with and cross over into art and design practice. In large part, craft histories of the Asia Pacific have been underrecognized in conversations about craft emerging from the industry and academic centers of the West, and yet the economic potential of handicraft- and craft-based social enterprise is quite visible in many Asian countries. Vietnam, in particular, has a very significant history of craft practices, with thousands of craft villages sustaining cultural practices and generating income for local communities. Craft villages have a centuries-long history and have been an integral part of the country's economic development, contributing 41% of GDP and employing 64% of the workforce in the industrial, nonstate sector in Vietnam in 1999 (Fanchette and Stedman 2018).

While rapid development, particularly in urban areas, has shifted the balance from handicrafts to commercial manufacturing in recent decades, there are still more than 2,000 craft villages operating in Vietnam today, as recognized by the government

(SRV 2018). These villages continue to provide important opportunities for income generation, particularly for rural communities, and support the retention of cultural practices and knowledge. Craft practices of note are handmade textiles such as specialized silk along with embroidery, weaving, and knitting practices; lacquer painting; ceramics; glass; production of recycled paper; furniture and woodcraft; and bamboo and rattan (Thi 2020). Craft aesthetics and craft cultures are a significant part of Vietnam's creative sector, as can be seen from contemporary art and design practice through to high fashion and youth street culture. This speaks to the power of craft to activate communities and its increasing interconnection with design and art cultures (Budge 2016).

Given the important role that craft plays in Vietnamese social, economic, and cultural development, there are growing concerns about the environmental impact, including pollution, generated through largely unregulated, semi-industrial craft practices, and, simultaneously, about the ongoing viability of craft villages amid rapid technological advancements and urban development agendas. Craft practices occupy an interesting position in terms of ecological sustainability—they have the potential both to address sustainability by privileging natural materials and methods and to contribute to environmental damage when not practiced with ecological care (Thi 2020). At the forefront of many emerging Vietnamese art, craft, and design practitioners' thinking, therefore, is how to collaborate with artisans and craft villages to sustain these important aspects of Vietnamese creative culture, while also connecting with contemporary global creative industries amid a time of ecological crisis. It is no coincidence that what is known as the "third wave" of craft globally has arisen in parallel to increasing concerns about environmental and social issues. As Kylie Budge argues, "People have responded to these concerns, and to those generated through mass global production, by literally taking matters into their own hands, and connecting with making on a deep level" (2016, 82). This observation resonates with the excitement and commitment that many young creatives in Vietnam and Australia are demonstrating toward craft practices.

Sustainability is therefore understood in this book in a multidimensional way—encompassing social and cultural goals (generating incomes for communities that need it, preserving important cultural heritage) alongside economic and environmental concerns (Demartini et al. 2021). This understanding draws on the extensive work of UNESCO in recent years to emphasize the multidimensional nature of sustainability and, in particular, the role of arts and culture in promoting different aspects of sustainable development (UNESCO 2023). In a recent UNESCO report, "Re|Shaping Policies for Creativity: Addressing Culture as a Global Public Good," Yarri Kamaro argues that the creative industries—including art, craft, and design as featured in this book—can and do support different pillars of sustainable development: "In national sustainable development planning, the cultural and creative sectors are recognized for their ability to advance cultural outcomes (65%) and drive societal transformations (63%), particularly in the realm of social inclusion. Resulting plans and strategies also harness the economic potential of the cultural and creative industries (54%), especially in developing countries" (UNESCO 2023, 209).

Economic development is supported by creative businesses that draw on local materials and skills that do not require large capital investment or complex infrastructure. Aspects of social development are supported through the community-building nature of creative and cultural practices. Environmental sustainability is supported through creative practices that make use of local, natural materials, including practices of recycling, upcyling, and reuse. As a result, UNESCO positions culture as a key part of sustainable development and advocates for greater awareness of the culture–environment nexus (UNESCO 2023).

This holistic approach to sustainability can be witnessed across communities in the Asia Pacific that are grappling with the impacts of climate change and rapid economic development. Rising sea levels are an especially concerning issue for Vietnam, with its low-lying coastal and river delta regions. It is also battling alarming levels of plastic waste and dangerously poor air-quality levels. The country's manufacturing sector, largely servicing consumer markets in other parts of the world, is a significant contributor to these problems. The need to find alternative pathways and visions of "development" has become particularly urgent. At the same time, in Australia, questions of social and cultural sustainability have come to the fore as we see seismic cultural shifts in the arts and creative industries with calls to address the legacies of colonization and recognize the important contributions, and struggles, of First Nations peoples (Smith 2021). These concerns with sustainability and decolonization are different in each country, shaping emergent connections between Vietnamese and Australian creatives—and a key motivator for the cross-cultural collaboration and learning that we profile in this book.

There is another important connection between Vietnam and Australia that underlies the research interests of this book: the social ties that were forged at the end of the Vietnam War, when more than 100,000 Vietnamese families relocated to Australia over two decades following the end of the war in 1975 (Refugee Council of Australia 2022). There are now around 300,000 people (or 1.6% of the Australian population) with Vietnamese ancestry living in Australia, with the Vietnamese language being the fifth most spoken (DFAT 2021). Artists and designers with Vietnamese backgrounds are part of an ever-growing cohort of diverse creatives in Australia, and the arts and cultural sectors in both countries are being shaped by new dynamics of global mobility and intercultural exchange. Several of our coauthors and research team members have personal experiences that connect with this history and the Vietnamese global diaspora.

As we argue, cross-cultural collaboration at its best involves reciprocal exchange and learning; at its worst, it can perpetuate colonial tropes and structures of appropriation, reinforcing outdated hierarchies stemming from the old binaries of West/East. It is through this lens that we center contemporary Vietnamese craft, art, and design for their potential to challenge and transform dominant and limited understandings of craft in Western discourses—in particular, the elitist view of "fine art" as superior to craft and design, or what can be argued is an arbitrary separation of art from craft (Held and Sealy Lineberry 2013), along with the added hierarchy of design over manufacture or "craft" (Kaufmann-Buhler et al. 2019). Challenging these concepts and approaches is part of a contemporary shift toward *de-Westernizing creative labor studies* (Alacovska and Gill 2019). This involves going beyond providing examples of different practices from/in non-Western countries and cultures and toward changing the way we think about and theorize creative practice, informed by non-Western knowledge systems.

We are interested, therefore, in how Vietnamese creatives bring together the creative, experimental, and transformative thinking inherent to contemporary art, with care for material process and practical applications of craft. Creative works, including art, craft, and design, are valued on a continuum, rather than in entrenched hierarchies, and these democratized approaches to artistic and creative practice offer a range of models to generate income and reach diverse audiences. In Australia, meanwhile, craft is fast becoming a central part of contemporary culture—with a rise in art–craft collaborations and the development of craft- and fashion-based social enterprises that are reframing the cultural practices of migrant and Indigenous communities as central, rather than peripheral, to contemporary culture (Harwood et al. 2023; Luckman and Andrew 2020). This reflects a broader reorientation toward sustainability and decolonization taking place in the creative industries globally.

In spite of the undeniable importance and strength of craft in contemporary creative cultures, creative industries have been disrupted in many ways in the wake of the COVID-19 pandemic—from the closure of established venues and interrupted supply chains to the economic impacts of lockdowns (UNESCO 2022). Workers in Vietnam's textile manufacturing industry felt these disturbances acutely, as thousands lost their jobs and suffered the impacts of diminished livelihoods (Ghosh and Kim 2021). These developments demanded a rethinking of how things are done—including shifts toward locally made production, more sustainable practices, and increasing digital literacy for creative practitioners. It was precisely this disruption that led to the case studies and opportunities for cross-cultural collaboration that are explored in this book. The *đây/đó (here/there)* project began with an online, international exhibition responding to the impact of extended COVID-19 restrictions and border closures in both Australia and Vietnam that lasted for almost two years. The lockdowns in Naarm/Melbourne were the longest in the world, totaling 262 days over 6 separate lockdown periods (Macreadie 2022). Meanwhile, in Saigon, severe limitations on mobility and access to food and basic provisions were overseen by the country's military. These difficult conditions prompted an urgent rethinking of how intercultural exchange and learning might be practiced.

Colleagues at Royal Melbourne Institute of Technology (RMIT)'s campuses in Naarm/Melbourne, Australia, and Hanoi and Ho Chi

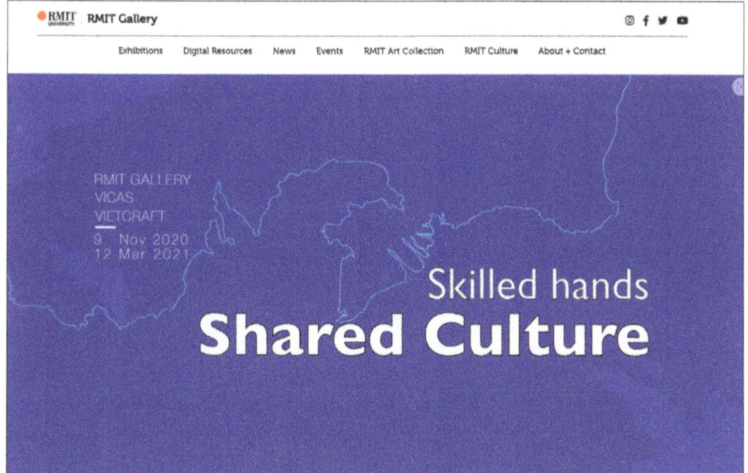

Figure 1.1. Screenshot of *Skilled Hands, Shared Culture* online exhibition.

Minh City, Vietnam, came together to build digital connections while creatives were working in isolation and to begin to unpack the shared interests in sustainability of craft, design, and art practitioners in both countries—during a time of shared global crisis. The resulting exhibition, titled *Skilled Hands, Shared Culture* (November 2020–March 2021), featured eight artists from Vietnam: Le Giang, Nguyễn Tấn Phát, Nguyễn Thị Dũng, Nguyễn Văn Lợi, Phạm Thị Ngọc Trâm, Thư Kim Vũ, Văn Ngô Trọng, and Vũ Thảo; it also featured eleven Australian artists/art collectives: Claire Tracey, Grace Lillian Lee, Lindy de Wijn, Michelle Hamer, Muhubo Salieman, Slow Art Collective (Dylan Martorell and Chaco Kato), Vermin (Lia Tabrah and Perina Drummond), Vicki Couzens, Vipoo Srivilasa, Yu Fang Chi, and Kieren Karritpul. The exhibition was cocurated by an Australian and Vietnamese team including industry partners Nguyễn Thị Thu Hà and Nguyễn Khoi from VICAS and Lê Bá Ngọc from Vietcraft; colleagues at RMIT

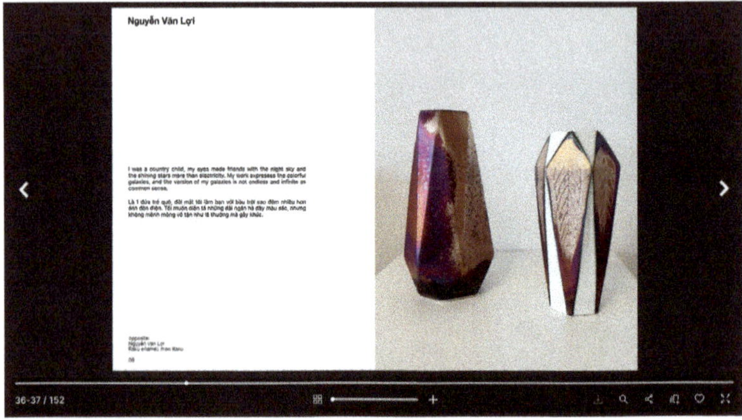

Figure 1.2. Detail of exhibition catalogue for *Skilled Hands, Shared Culture* online exhibition.

Culture, including Helen Rayment, Evelyn Tsitas, and Monica Do; and the authors of this book.

Skilled Hands, Shared Culture was the starting point for the development of a larger, longer-term project titled *đây/đó (here/there)*, which asks a number of questions: How can creative practices adapt to major disruptions such as the global pandemic or climate catastrophes? How can creatives in Australia and Vietnam, with shared interests in sustainable craft practices, learn from each other? Can cross-cultural collaboration in the craft, art, and design sectors support sustainable development in a holistic sense? Our understanding of cross-cultural collaboration draws from critical studies of Western imperialism and colonization, including the work of Linda Tuhiwai Smith, Eve Tuck, and, as previously discussed, Catherine Walsh and Walter Mignolo—accepting that we are working within colonial structures, addressing power imbalances in cross-cultural research, and thinking about ways that Indigenous and/or marginalized ethnic communities will

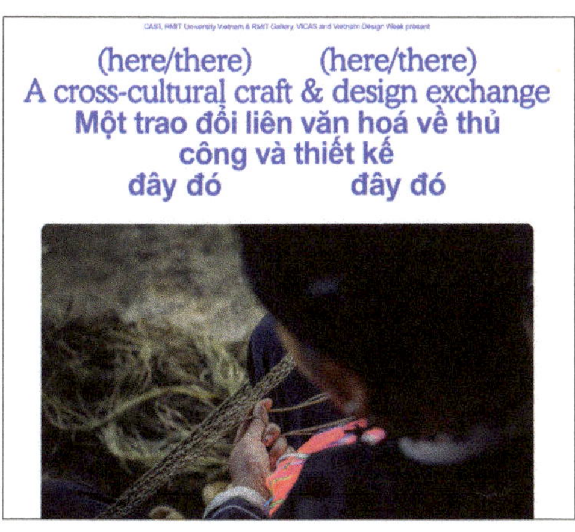

Figure 1.3. *đây/đó (here/there)* website.

tangibly benefit from the research (Mignolo and Walsh 2018; Smith 2021; Tuck 2009).

From 2021 to 2023, the *đây/đó (here/there)* project responded to these questions by supporting creative practice and collaboration. It has facilitated a number of practical, creative projects featuring emerging designers in Vietnam who share a passion for sustainable craft practices, collaborating with industry mentors in Vietnam and Australia to create new work and reach new and diverse audiences. We have worked closely with Nguyễn Thị Thu Hà in developing the creative collaborations. The four case studies featured in this book are collaborations with Vietnamese creatives—Lưu Như Ngọc, Đàm Nhã Hân, Phạm Phan Hoàng Linh, and Tom Trandt Minh Đạo—working at the intersection of craft, art, and design. They each participated in a long-term cross-cultural mentorship with industry professionals in Australia and Vietnam to extend and develop their creative practices, with a particular view to sustainable design and cultural heritage. All four were finalists in Vietnam Design Week

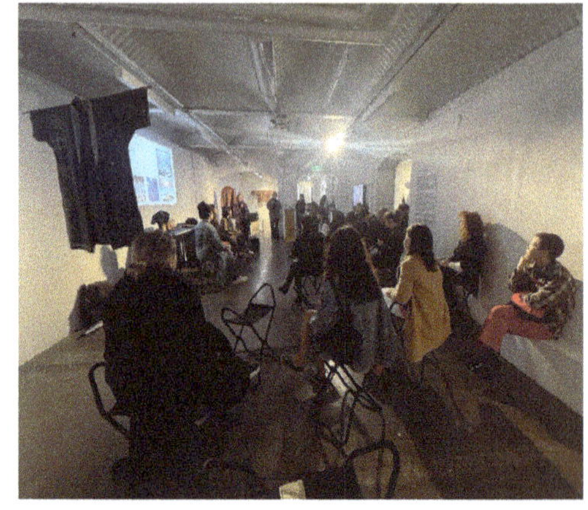

Figure 1.4. Artist talk by Phạm Phan Hoàng Linh and Tom Trandt Minh Đạo for Melbourne Fashion Week 2023, with Hoang Hong Hanh as translator for Linh. Courtesy of Becky Lu.

2021, an annual festival that celebrates local design talent across the lifestyle, fashion, public art, tourism, and food industries.

In addition to these four case studies, the project has encompassed workshops, talks, exhibitions, and international residencies. Importantly, the project has encouraged a "slow" methodology that privileges long-term collaboration and the development of reciprocal relationships that will last over time. By delving into these case studies in the following chapters, we aim to highlight innovative craft practices in the Asia Pacific that challenge hierarchies of value in traditional art, craft, and design discourses and signal toward decolonial methods in creative practice research.

Chapter 2 focuses on the work of two fashion and textile practitioners. Phạm Phan Hoàng Linh operates a vertical craft and design studio in the Sa Pa region in the north of Vietnam, collaborating with local ethnic minority artisans to create carefully crafted fashion, design, and handicraft pieces made from locally sourced plant fibers and hand-dyed with natural materials. Tom Trandt Minh Đạo, the founder of Saigon-based fashion label Môi Điên, works with craft techniques to upcycle remnant fabrics sourced from the city's textile factories into new contemporary fashion items. Linh and Tom benefited from exchanges with a number of creative professionals from fashion and craft enterprises, including Vũ Thảo of Kilomet109 in Vietnam, Dewi Cooke from The Social Studio in Australia, and James Bartle from Outland Denim in Australia. Both case studies highlight the shifting meanings of heritage and sustainability when working cross-culturally—whether this is through the exchange of design knowledge across countries, between youth subcultures and emerging fashion trends, or between Indigenous and non-Indigenous communities. Linh and Tom also explore new ideas for commercializing their practice and developing sustainable

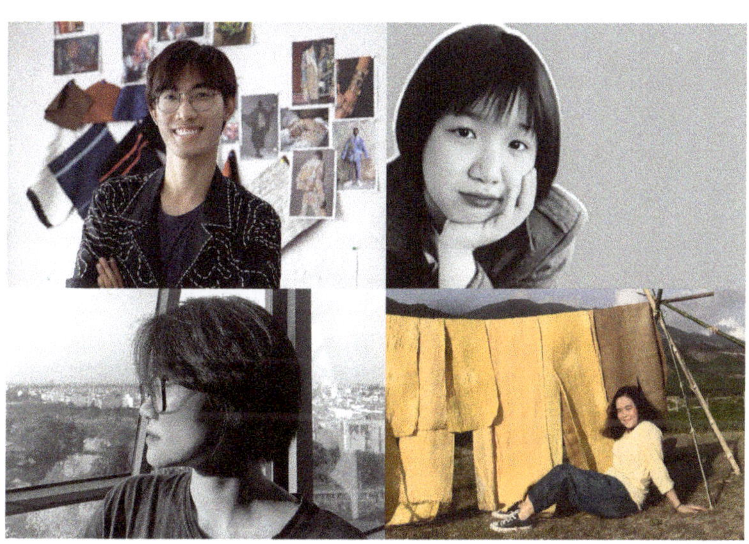

Figure 1.5. Clockwise from top left: Tom Trandt Minh Đạo, Lưu Như Ngọc, Phạm Phan Hoàng Linh, and Đàm Nhã Hân. The four creatives featured in the case studies. Courtesy of the artists.

business models that privilege craft methods and build on growing social enterprise and social business movements globally.

In chapter 3, we turn to other kinds of material practice, including ceramics and woodworking/furniture design. We look at the work of two emerging practitioners, Lưu Như Ngọc and Đàm Nhã Hân, who share a passion for craft traditions and cultural heritage in Vietnam. Lưu Như Ngọc worked with upcycling techniques to transform ceramic waste into new artworks. In doing so, she supports the ongoing work of the Bát Tràng ceramic village and the Temple of Literature—drawing attention to the community importance of these sites and histories. Đàm Nhã Hân's practice, meanwhile, celebrates Vietnamese architectural heritage through industrial design, working with local makers to produce contemporary furniture that honors rural architecture, in particular the three-room or *ba gian* house. In both practices, traditional hierarchies of design are destabilized to foreground the importance of material process and craft histories in developing new work that is culturally relevant while engaging with contemporary audiences. These two practitioners worked with a range of industry professionals to extend their ideas and practices, including Vietnamese craft advocate Lê Bá Ngọc and managing editor of *Elle Decoration Vietnam* Nguyễn Phan Thuỳ Dương, alongside Australian mentors, including furniture designer Dale Hardiman of Dowel Jones furniture, ceramicist Jennifer Conroy-Smith, and design lecturer Ronnie Lacham.

Each of the case studies that we profile reflects cross-cultural encounters between

Australian and Vietnamese practitioners with shared goals of drawing from and celebrating craft. They each demonstrate the importance of experimentation and adaptation in working toward sustainability in the creative industries, framing sustainability as a "work in progress" rather than a fixed end goal. They also highlight the challenges of intercultural exchange and the need to be attentive to the institutional conditions and relationships that shape creative outcomes. Chapter 4 unpacks these challenges and our own learnings as researchers and creatives in both countries seeking to promote reciprocal learning.

We articulate these possibilities as a kind of "craft futurism." Craft is often regarded as a nostalgic idea, connected to practices and traditions from the past. The Western idea of craft emerged in the mid-nineteenth century as the "other" of industrial manufacturing, recognizing the role of human, haptic skill and nonmechanical labor in the production of unique goods (Luckman and Thomas 2018). Craft or artisanal work is thus still understood in terms of a particular temporality that resists capitalist time and offers alternative ways of being in the world. These aspects of craft have been taken up in "craftivist" movements circulating in the West that promote anti-capitalist and inclusive forms of community building and public intervention (Clarke 2016; Greer 2014). In this book, we offer the rubric of craft futurism as a similarly progressive idea, but one that encompasses non-Western creative practices—particularly their dynamic processes of adaptation and ongoing vitality through cross-cultural exchange. We argue that such an affirmative understanding of adaptation can help to counter the legacies of colonialism, appropriation, whitewashing, and the unequal global distribution of labor that still shapes the craft and fashion sectors worldwide (Almila and Delice 2023; Patel 2020).

Like other arts and literary futurisms, craft futurism is a speculative idea linked to a critical social or political agenda (Guffey 2014; Mauer 2021). Yet, unlike futurisms or avant-gardisms that involve a disconnection or severing from "tradition," craft futurism emphasizes the connections between cultural memory and inherited connections to the land that offer resources for working toward more sustainable and regenerative futures.

These interdependencies between past, present, and future are central to our agenda. In Vietnam, craft involves practices of making that emerge from the hereditary knowledge of a diverse array of fifty-four officially recognized ethnic and Indigenous groups. These practices have been hybridized, adapted, and threatened through successive waves of colonization. In Vietnam, as in many other Asian countries, the durability of these practices has involved not resisting, but participating in markets and entrepreneurial activity that can support cultural sustainability. Two of the *đây/đó* mentees already run craft-based fashion businesses, while the others aspire to economic success from their craft and design practices. This points to the need for a future-oriented discourse that can *connect* the economic, cultural, social, and ecological possibilities of craft. Of particular interest is how we can think beyond a narrow concept of cultural sustainability as preservation of the past toward one that can accommodate design innovation, market engagement, cross-cultural exchange, and the strengthening of local cultural knowledge. In this respect, craft futurism reflects a "transformational" rather than "backwards looking" agenda (Mauer 2021, 613) that seeks to avoid romanticizing non-Western cultures and the maintenance of "tradition."

Such an orientation involves defining culture as complexity and interdependence. We ask how contemporary kinds of mobility—experienced by Vietnamese craft practitioners and creatives through travel, education, online media, and cultural consumption—converge with "tradition" and longstanding ecological practices. Our mentees' encounters with their mentors and their participation in exhibitions and presentations of their work in Vietnam and Australia have involved exploratory and speculative modes of making, learning, and adapting to diverse contexts. As researchers and scholars, we have also learned from these engagements and experienced how they offer new ways of imagining our cultural and ecological futures. We are attentive to both the limits and the possibilities of cross-cultural collaborations and how they can guide us toward new understandings of craft, creativity, and sustainability in a culturally complex and interconnected world.

References

Alacovska, A., and R. Gill. 2019. "De-Westernizing Creative Labour Studies: The Informality of Creative Work from an Ex-Centric Perspective." *International Journal of Cultural Studies* 22 (2): 195–212.

Almila, A. M., and S. Delice, eds. 2023. *Fashion's Transnational Inequalities: Socio-Political, Economic, and Environmental.* Taylor & Francis.

Ang, Ien. 2011. "Navigating Complexity: From Cultural Critique to Cultural Intelligence." *Continuum* 25 (6): 779–94.

Budge, K. 2016. "The 'New' Craft Phenomena and the Contemporary Museum." *Craft Research* 7 (1): 79–89.

Clarke, K. 2016. "Willful Knitting? Contemporary Australian Craftivism and Feminist Histories." *Continuum* 30 (3): 298–306.

Demartini, P., L. Marchegiani, M. Marchiori, and G. Schiuma. 2021. "Connecting the Dots: A Proposal to Frame the Debate Around Cultural Initiatives and Sustainable Development." In *Cultural Initiatives for Sustainable Development*, edited by P. Demartini, L. Marchegiani, M. Marchiori, and G. Schiuma. Contributions to Management Science. Springer.

Department of Foreign Affairs and Trade, Australian Federal Government. 2021. "Australia–Vietnam Enhanced Economic Engagement Strategy." Accessed November 10, 2023. https://www.dfat.gov.au/australia-vietnam/eees/en/index.html.

Duxbury, N., and M. Jeannotte. 2011. "Introduction: Culture and Sustainable Communities". In *Culture and Local Governance / Culture et gouvernance locale* 3 (1–2): 1–10. https://doi.org/10.18192/clg-cgl.v3i1.181.

Fanchette, S., and N. Stedman. 2018. *Discovering Craft Villages in Vietnam: Ten Itineraries around Hà Nội.* IRD Éditions.

Ghosh, S., and M. Kim. 2021. "Vietnam Factories Short of Workers After Heavy-Handed Lockdowns – Cento Ventures." *Reuters*. Accessed December 27, 2023. https://www.reuters.com/markets/funds/vietnam-factories-short-workers-after-heavy-handed-lockdowns-cento-ventures-2021-12-02/.

Greer, B., ed. 2014. *Craftivism: The Art of Craft and Activism*. Arsenal Pulp Press.

Guffey, Elizabeth. 2014. "Crafting Yesterday's Tomorrows: Retro-Futurism, Steampunk, and the Problem of Making in the Twenty-First Century." *Journal of Modern Craft* 7 (3): 249–66.

Harwood, T., G. McQuilten, and A. White. 2023. *Variations: A More Diverse Picture of Contemporary Art*. Monash University Publishing.

Kaufmann-Buhler, Jennifer, Victoria Rose Pass, and Christopher Wilson, eds. 2019. *Design History Beyond the Canon*. Bloomsbury Publishing USA.

Khan, R. 2023. "The Sociality of Decolonisation: Making Fashion, Heritage, and Cultural Sustainability in Vietnam." In *Fashion's Transnational Inequalities: Socio-Political, Economic, and Environmental*, edited by A. M. Almila and S. Delice. Routledge.

Luckman, S., and J. Andrew. 2020. *Craftspeople and Designer Makers in the Contemporary Creative Economy*. Springer Nature. https://doi.org/10.1007/978-3-030-44979-7.

Luckman, S., and N. Thomas. 2018. *Craft Economies*. Bloomsbury.

Mauer, K. W. 2021. "Unsettling Resilience: Colonial Ecological Violence, Indigenous Futurisms, and the Restoration of the Elwha River." *Rural Sociology* 86 (3): 611–34.

Macreadie, Ian. 2022. "Reflections from Melbourne, the World's Most Locked-Down City, through the COVID-19 Pandemic and Beyond." In *Microbiology Australia* 43 (1): 3–4.

Mignolo, Walter D., and Catherine E. Walsh. 2018. *On Decoloniality: Concepts, Analytics, Praxis*. Duke University Press.

Patel, K. 2020. "Diversity Initiatives and Addressing Inequalities in Craft." In *Pathways Into Creative Working Lives*, edited by S. Taylor and S. Luckman. Springer Nature.

Refugee Council of Australia. 2022. "How Do Refugees Come to Australia Under Its Refugee and Humanitarian Program?" Accessed December 27, 2023. https://www.refugeecouncil.org.au/coming-to-australia/6/.

Sealy Lineberry, H., and Held, P., eds. 2013. *Crafting a Continuum: Rethinking Contemporary Craft*. University of North Carolina Press.

Smith, L. T. 2021. *Decolonizing Methodologies: Research and Indigenous Peoples*. Bloomsbury Academic & Professional.

[SRV] Socialist Republic of Vietnam. 2018. Decree on Development of Rural Crafts, no. 52/2018/ND-CP Hanoi, April 12.

Thi, L. N. 2020. *Environmental Pollution in Vietnam's Craft Villages*. EDP Sciences.

Tuck, E. 2009. "Suspending Damage: A Letter to Communities." *Harvard Educational Review* 79 (3): 409–27.

[UNESCO] United Nations Educational, Scientific and Cultural Organization. 2022. "Assessment of the Impact of COVID-19 on Cultural and Creative Industries." Accessed September 15, 2023. https://unesdoc.unesco.org/ark:/48223/pf0000382281.

[UNESCO] United Nations Educational, Scientific and Cultural Organization. 2023. "Re|Shaping Policies for Creativity: Addressing Culture as a Global Public Good." Accessed December 27, 2023. https://unesdoc.unesco.org/ark:/48223/pf0000380474.

CHAPTER TWO

Experiments in Sustainability: Vietnamese Craft and Design for Contemporary Fashion Markets

The two case studies featured in this chapter are part of a global movement of creative businesses that are pursuing sustainability goals by drawing on craft practices and ethics. We consider the role of craft in contributing to, and disrupting, the dominant sustainability logic in fashion and the idea of sustainable design as experimentation, adaptation, and work in progress. Sustainable fashion is a consumer trend, a material practice, and a creative and ethical ideal that is fraught with contradiction. While there is reportedly wide public support for a more sustainable fashion industry (D'Arpizio et al. 2020), consumers are also buying fashion in greater quantities and more cheaply than ever before. There are hundreds of fashion brands describing their garments as "sustainable," "eco," "conscious," or "responsible," but many still contribute to systems of overproduction and consumption that generate huge volumes of waste, contributing to growing claims of "greenwashing" (Baptist World Aid 2021; Shendruk 2022). The dyeing and processing of synthetic textiles causes major ecological damage, polluting rivers and waterways in the places where fashion is mass-produced, out of view from the urban centers in which most of the world's textiles are consumed. Fashion commentators and scholars hold differing opinions on what sustainability in fashion entails—from avoiding "fast fashion" brands, embracing thrifting and vintage resale platforms, consuming less, or investing in clothing made from natural fibers and circular design principles (Fletcher 2016; Gwilt 2013; Payne 2019). Sustainable fashion can encompass practices of reuse, making, and mending; design and material innovations; and alternative supply chain structures. Understood in these broad terms, sustainable fashion involves a wide range of experimentation with textile processes, business models, and labor practices.

Craft plays a key role within these sustainability experiments. By its nature, craft supports material processes and business practices that align with slower and scaled-down systems of textile production. These practices can challenge capitalist ideals of growth and expansion, while still offering tactile pleasures and social and cultural value. Our two case studies in this chapter include the work of Phạm Phan Hoàng Linh and Tom Trandt Minh Đạo, who both apply historical artisanal knowledge to produce textiles that are future-oriented. They illustrate, in very different ways, how craft can involve processes of creative reinvention that contribute to cultural sustainability. We invoke the idea of cultural sustainability not simply to mean cultural preservation, but to signal a more relational and dynamic process of ongoing cultural adaptation. Both Linh's and Tom's fashion making highlight these interconnections between past, present, and future and how they become realized within transnational or "more than local" fashion markets (Khan 2021).

Sustainability is a provocation to which both designers respond through their diverse approaches to the sourcing and manipulation of fibers, dyes, cuts, and embellishments. We suggest that instead of defining sustainability as a static goal defined by a fixed and stable set of criteria, it is more usefully understood as an evolving and iterative set of practices. The idea of "sustainability as experiment" foregrounds the material and cultural contexts in which Linh and Tom work, their ongoing efforts to test out and develop sustainability practices. We describe how both designers innovate and adapt craft processes that are aimed at durability, minimizing waste, and finding alternatives to synthetic materials and chemicals. These are not perfect processes, and the designers' work reflects how creatives *learn* to be sustainable, through experimentation and knowledge exchange.

In this chapter, we discuss their work within the local context of Vietnam and share how we came to know this work through a transcultural mentoring process. In doing so, we share some reflections on creativity, mobility, and the possibilities of cultural exchange.

Sustainability Experiments: Linht Handicraft

Linht Handicraft is a small boutique in the outskirts of Sa Pa, a resort town in the mountainous northern provinces of Vietnam. The store is not easy to find. Motorbike taxis from the center of Sa Pa take tourists to the gates of Cat Cat, a model village where visitors can

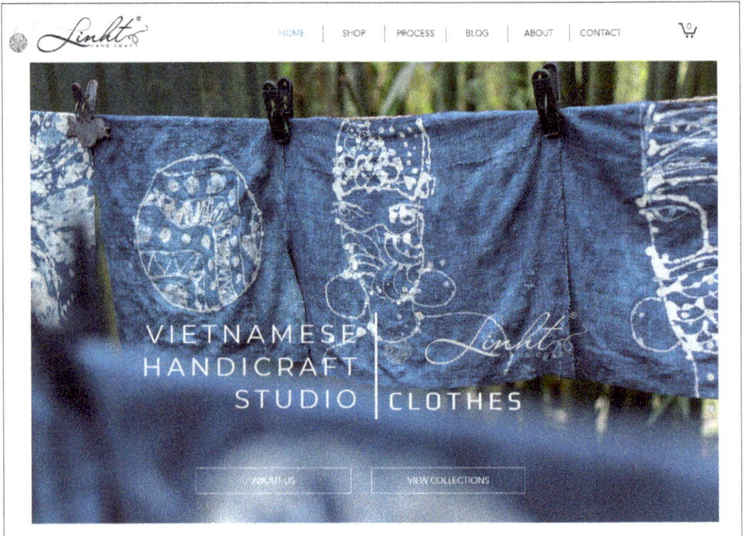

Figure 2.1. Linht Handicraft website, 2023.

experience rural life as practiced by the local H'mong people, one of fifty-four officially recognized ethnic minority groups in Vietnam. The H'mong ethnic group is indigenous to highland areas across Vietnam, also residing in other Southeast Asian countries, including Laos, Thailand, Myanmar, and China. In Vietnam, they are famed for their distinctive, brightly colored embroidery. Their textiles are a major tourist commodity in Sa Pa, and it is common to see local and foreign visitors trying on and photographing themselves in H'mong attire and headgear. From the entrance to Cat Cat, a steep and narrow lane leads to Linh's boutique. It stands out from other shops in the area, many of which offer the same H'mong souvenirs and costumes available for tourists to buy or rent. Inside a wooden stilt house, Linht Handicraft offers a more muted and bohemian atmosphere. The shop is adorned with hemp and cotton fabrics dyed in many shades of indigo. Kimonos featuring wax batik designs hang from the ceiling, while brightly colored paintings present visitors with stylized depictions of Sa Pa life.

The cooler climate and dramatic vistas in this region make it a popular holiday destination. The area is dotted with a growing number of luxury hotels that contrast with the surrounding rice terraces and rural mountain life. The local handicraft industry, in which ethnic minority groups such as the H'mong have participated for decades, is reliant on this tourist economy. While the region is slowly recovering from the border closures and impacts of the COVID-19 pandemic, its growing tourist infrastructure is poorly regulated, posing serious risks to local communities and ecologies (Nguyen et al. 2023).

Phạm Phan Hoàng Linh has lived in Sa Pa for nearly a decade. She was born and raised in the countryside in Quảng Nam and studied fine art at Huế University in central Vietnam. Linh says that during field trips to the northern highlands, she fell in love with the scenery and the local people. After graduating, she decided to move to Sa Pa with her husband. Both artists, they felt at home among the hills and found inspiration in this idyllic village life:

> The images of women and girls embroidering on the porch, poles of cloth drying in the sun, hands spinning flax, floating clouds, rays of sunlight on the tops of trees . . . these images are enough to catch my heart. And they are the bridge that brought me to a career that is completely unrelated to what I was trained in, dyeing, sewing and designing. I learned to dye

indigo and draw beeswax from H'mong women and friends to satisfy my passion and emotions. I use my personal feelings as an artist to make fashion, to play with colours. (*đây/đó: here/there* 2023)

After moving to Sa Pa in 2014, Linh and her husband decided to start a business selling her artwork. Years of living alongside local H'mong people allowed her to observe and learn from their way of life and their natural dyeing techniques, so she expanded her interest from painting to creating textiles. Linh began creating designs using the local beeswax batik technique. Her identity as an artist evolved as she developed intimate bonds with H'mong women. She started selling coats, scarves, dresses, and blouses made from locally sourced hemp and cotton[3] and mottled with the dark blue of indigo, rust, and pink hues derived from yam root and the amber of celandine. The distinctive patterns come from Japanese *shibori* dyeing methods, giving Linh's textiles an aesthetic identity that resonates with both local and foreign customers.

Linh's project for the *đây/đó (here/there)* mentorship was *Rẻo*, a concept design for a range of upcycled hats. Made from indigo-dyed scrap fabric, the hats could be converted into bags, reflecting both simplicity and versatility (Vietnam Design Week 2020). Linh's design caught our attention for its commitment to sustainability and for her enthusiasm for local craft and artisanship. Linh worked with two mentors—Dewi Cooke, the CEO of Melbourne-based The Social Studio (TSS), and Vũ Thảo, the founder and design director of sustainable fashion brand

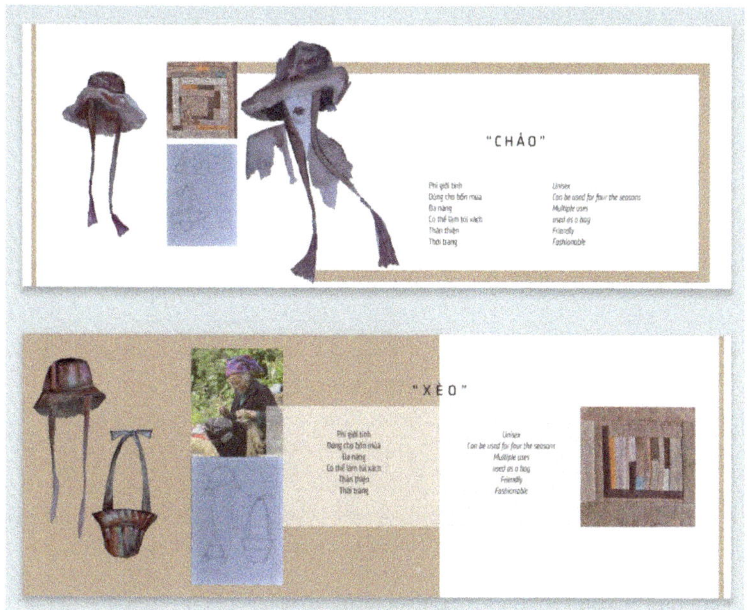

Figure 2.2. Phạm Phan Hoàng Linh's *Rẻo* proposal for Vietnam Design Week 2021. Courtesy of Phạm Phan Hoàng Linh.

Kilomet109. Thảo is a well-known figure in Hanoi's creative scene, and her brand has been widely featured in the local and international fashion press, exhibitions, and symposia. Since its launch in 2012, Kilomet109 has become known for its distinctive blend of contemporary design and traditional Vietnamese craftsmanship. Over this period, Thảo has built relationships with a number of Indigenous and ethnic minority communities in different parts of Vietnam, who contribute their weaving, dyeing, batik, and embroidery techniques. Through these collaborations, Thảo adapts local heritage for contemporary luxury markets. TSS is a nonprofit social enterprise that provides educational and vocational opportunities to people from refugee and new migrant communities in Melbourne. TSS trains students in apparel design and construction and is an Ethical Clothing Australia–accredited manufacturer and socially conscious retailer. It participates in creative projects ranging from Melbourne Fashion Week collaborations with local artists and designers to more community-focused events.

Online meetings between Linh, her mentors, and the *đây/đó (here/there)* researchers took place for a year, leading to an online project showcase in November 2022. During these meetings, Linh would speak in detail about her creative ideas and works in progress. She shared concept sketches and designs for a new line of bags and hats incorporating new materials, techniques, and collaborations. We were interested to hear

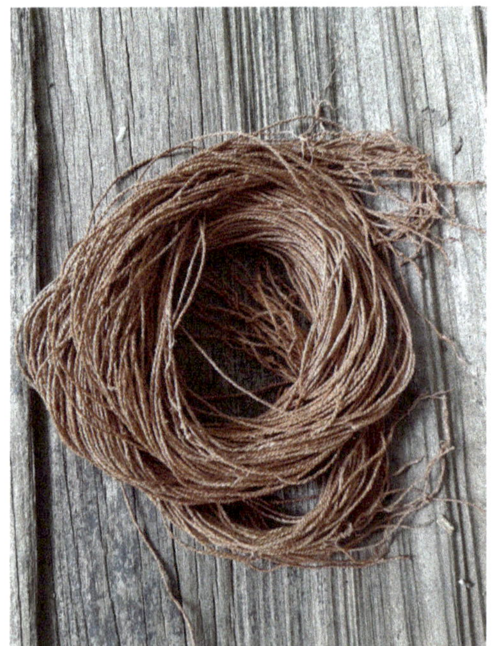

Figure 2.3. Detail of ramie fibers. Courtesy of Phạm Phan Hoàng Linh.

about Linh's explorations with ramie, a plant that is native to China and Southeast Asia. It is used for food, medicine, and yarn. Its durability, strength, and luster have made it popular for use in textiles in this region for centuries (Angelini and Taverini 2013). Linh explained how ramie is an ancient fiber that was used to make fishing nets in Vietnam, and in times of war, it was used to make ropes for boats. It is stronger than hemp but also becomes softer with use. Given these historical applications, there is significant potential for its use in contemporary fashion and textile markets.

Linh learned about ramie from Dao Tuyển women who live in villages in Lao Cai, near the border with China. The Dao community is another "ethnic minority group"

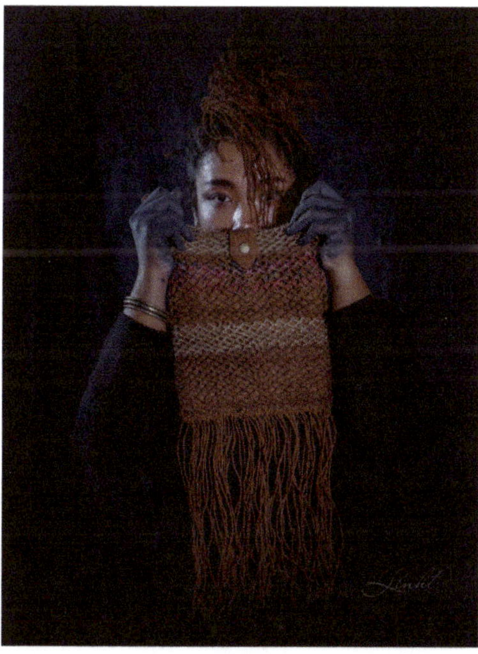

Figure 2.4. Phạm Phan Hoàng Linh bag design featuring ramie fibers. Dyed with yam root. Courtesy of Phạm Phan Hoàng Linh.

with roots in Vietnam reported to go back to the thirteenth century (Tung et al. 2023). Dao Tuyển people used locally grown ramie to make bags, although increasingly these have been replaced with bags made from nylon. The bags are produced by painstakingly knotting ramie fibers. Linh had heard about these processes and decided to travel to a Dao Tuyển village to learn more about their craft. She visited a family who grew a small quantity of ramie for their own use. She was inspired to collaborate with Dao Tuyển women and use ramie to produce her own line of bags. They dried and then spent many hours twisting and knotting the plant fibers to create a twine that is then dyed and used to construct the bags. Linh used a crocheting technique her aunt taught her as a child that resembled the knotting methods she observed among Dao Tuyển women. Together, it takes Linh and the women around a month to produce crocheted ramie fabric for one bag. Producing the bags is just one of many livelihood activities for the Dao Tuyển community, so they work on it between other tasks. Linh mentioned that she was excited to grow the product line—if she can scale up production, then she can contribute to the future livelihood of these communities.

There was other experimentation with sustainable methods that went into the making of the bags. Linh used indigo dye to create a blue ramie bag, while yam root produced a terra-cotta brown. She informed us that these colors get darker with time and use. We particularly liked one bag that was dyed a bright pink, but Linh informed us that the reason for this striking color was that she had used a chemical rather than a natural dye.

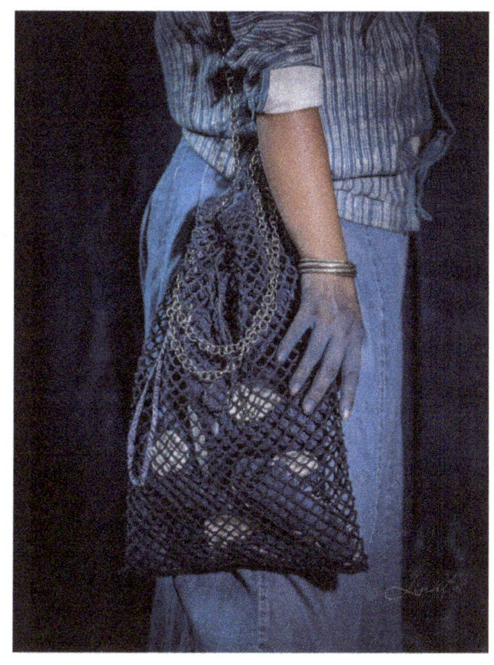

Figure 2.5. Indigo-dyed ramie-fiber bag. Courtesy of Phạm Phan Hoàng Linh.

She is still experimenting with natural pink dyes—sappanwood and shellac create pink and red hues, but these are not as intense or as long-lasting as she would like. Some of the prototypes were also embellished with H'mong embroidered scrap fabrics and jewelry. She had other ideas for incorporating upcycled materials, such as mixing ramie with leftover thread from H'mong tassels or attaching H'mong silver jewelry. She liked the idea of combining H'mong textiles with the Dao Tuyển crocheting styles to create something culturally distinctive. Some bags were adorned with metal chains that, although they added color and interest, were not "natural," upcycled, or necessarily sustainable. In this way, her creative process reflected a tension between creative freedom and

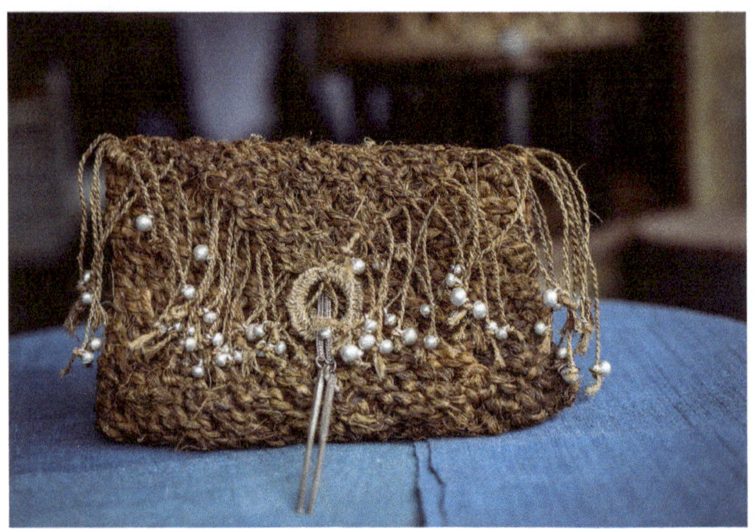

Figure 2.6. Ramie bag, woven with metal accessories from H'mong and Red Dao artists in Sa Pa. Courtesy of Phạm Phan Hoàng Linh.

sustainability, as well as ongoing learning and adaptation.

With the encouragement of her mentors, Linh started documenting and sharing photos and videos of these processes and collaborations with Dao Tuyển women, especially the elaborate knotting technique. This was not something Linh had foregrounded so explicitly before. While the culture and craftsmanship of Vietnam's ethnic minority groups are key to the country's creative industries, there is relatively little understanding of this ethnic diversity and a continuing marginalization and exoticization of many of these communities. There is a need to raise awareness of the creative value chain in Vietnam through more meaningful engagement and collaboration between local creatives and diverse communities—which is embodied in Linh's deep, long-term, and relational approach to working with local artisans. Dewi, drawing on her experience with TSS, suggested that Linh place greater emphasis on storytelling and foregrounding her collaborations with local communities:

> Linh shows herself to be somebody who has wonderful community connections in her work, and I can see how valuable that is for her and the way she wants to exist within the fashion landscape in Vietnam. So I think what would be so exciting is to see the ways she's trying to honour and bring to the forefront this traditional craftmanship and artisanship that she sees in her region in Sa Pa. From communities that aren't necessarily given that platform in a design sense as much. I would hope to see that extend beyond this project, and that she continues to find inspiration with those craftspeople and continues to work with them to elevate the beauty of what they do and how they create together. (*đây/đó: here/there* 2023)

The processes involved in making her bags, with this slower and more laborious method of weaving natural fibers with the Dao Tuyển community, were obviously more elaborate than Linh's previous work. This meant that there was the potential to promote the bags as a more "elevated" product—but doing so would require educating consumers about the process of making the bags, along with their cultural context.

These mentoring exchanges allowed Linh to develop a more astute understanding of the connections between cultural and economic value. Emphasizing the artisanal knowledge of Vietnam's diverse communities

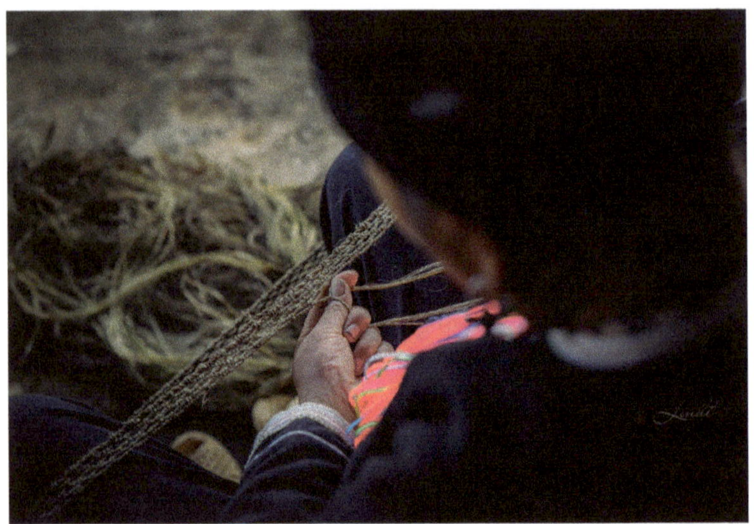

Figure 2.7. Detail of video by Phạm Phan Hoàng Linh documenting local Dao Tuyển artists weaving ramie fibers.

has been a consistent focus of Vũ Thảo and her brand Kilomet109. Thảo saw the use of locally sourced fibers and materials as a real strength in Linh's work: "I immediately think about the eco-friendly and the craft elements in her design process. Linh knows how to weave the abundant natural, local materials and the local resources into each designs. I can clearly see Linh's deep love for handmade materials through everything she packs into this project" (*đây/đó: here/there* 2023).

As a result of Linh's participation in the mentorship, her website and social media content have been updated to reflect this advice, sharing more about the brand's story and its engagement with local communities of artisans. Linht Handicraft's sustainability work now encompasses these knowledge-sharing efforts, as well as the material processes of fashion making in which Linh has long been engaged. The mentoring process has been key to imparting these kinds

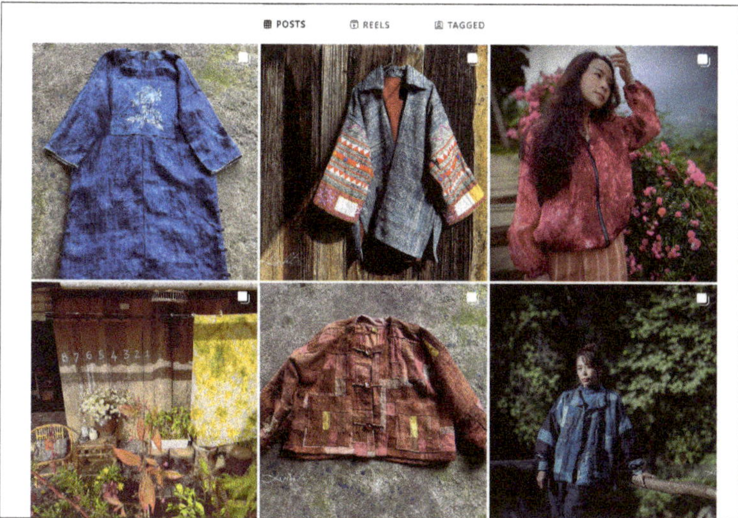

Figure 2.8. Screenshot of Linht Handicraft Instagram, December 29, 2023.

of business and marketing strategies that can support Linh's creative and sustainability efforts. As Linh reflects, "In the future, I think the products made from natural materials will win the hearts of consumers. The cross-cultural collaboration in Here/There is providing opportunities to exchange and learn from each other, to design and make a business out of it. To share our stories and show each other the best of our skills" (*đây/đó: here/there* 2023).

Môi Điên:
Urban Fashion Meets Craft

A counterpoint to Linh's poetic focus on craft heritage and slow living can be found in the work of Tom Trandt Minh Đạo and his urban fashion label, Môi Điên Studio. While Tom's studio shares Linh's interests in artisanal production and Vietnamese culture, his work has a much more urban and youth focus. Môi Điên translates into English as "mad lips" or "outspoken," and it captures the bright, energetic, and irreverent aspects of his creative practice. Born and raised in Saigon, Tom graduated from the New School Parsons School for Design, New York, in 2016, obtaining a BFA in fashion design. He returned to Saigon and launched his own label, Môi Điên Studio, shortly afterward. Tom's design process is characterized by a playful and experimental nature, which reflects his position as an emerging designer in the local fashion scene. By utilizing his experience studying overseas and drawing on his generational upbringing, Tom has found opportunities in everyday practices within Vietnam's textile industry to build his creative practice and respond to his environment. His design studio was founded in 2016 and quickly gained popularity due to its bold designs and environmentally conscious approach. More than just a fashion label, Môi Điên Studio soon developed into a hub for Saigon's style-conscious youth culture. The brand has hundreds of thousands of social media followers, and Tom has been profiled in many local fashion platforms, including *Elle Vietnam*, *L'Officiel*, *Hive Live*, *Saigoneer*, and others. While Môi Điên is very

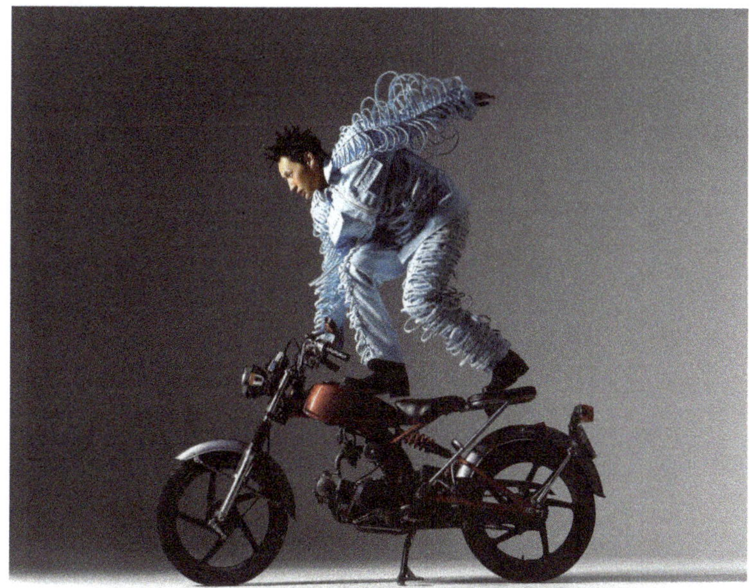

Figure 2.9. Image for Môi Điên lookbook featuring motorcycle jacket and pants with textile detailing. Courtesy of Tom Trandt Minh Đạo.

much a product of Tom's creative vision, he describes his process as a collaborative one, working closely with his team of designers as they experiment with deadstock fabrics sourced from the many textile factories on the outskirts of the city.

Vietnam's rapid economic growth over the last three decades has been driven by its role as a major garment manufacturer and exporter (Anh 2021; Hall 2021). However, it has been suggested that the development of this skill base in manufacturing has effectively positioned Vietnam at the "low value" end of the fashion industry, prompting calls to invest in higher-value activity such as design and marketing (Tran 2012, 134). Tom's creative strategy effectively subverts this positioning. By sourcing, reusing, and reinventing deadstock fabrics from these

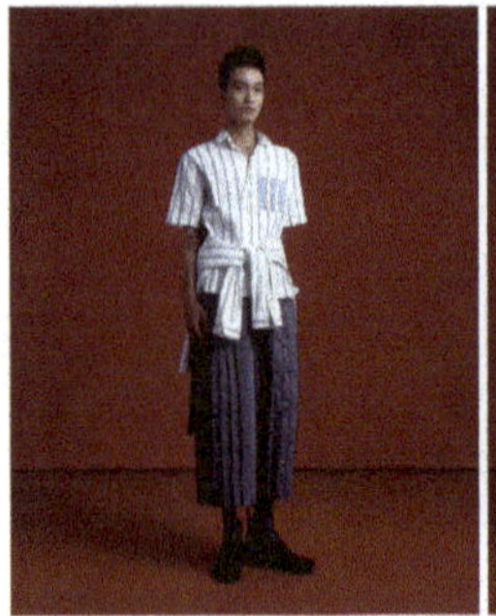

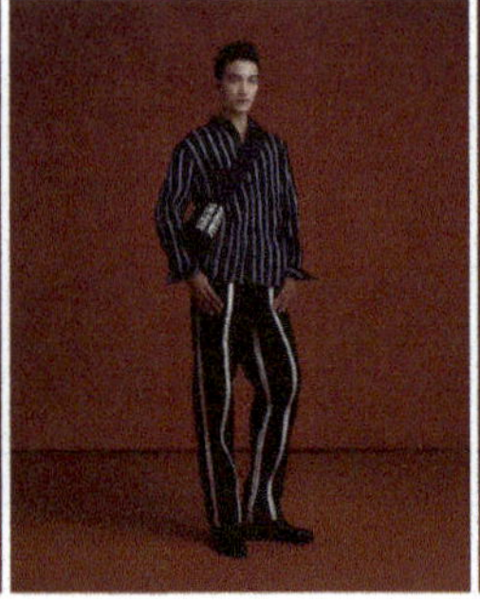

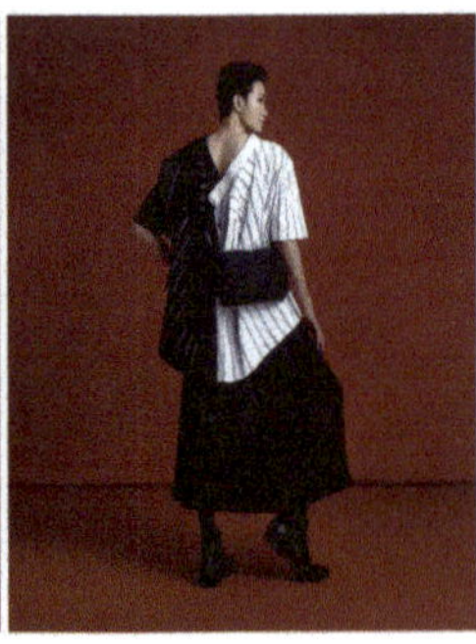

Figure 2.10. Screenshot of Môi Điên–Saigon SS 2024 Collection.

factories and subcontractors and turning them into cutting-edge garments for a newly emerging youth consumer market, he overturns this manufacture–design hierarchy and resituates Vietnam as a site of creative innovation. Saigon is a densely populated city of around nine million people. Around one-third of Vietnam's population is under the age of twenty-five (UN Vietnam 2013). Each night, thousands of young people gather at streetside coffee shops and traverse the city on their motorbikes. Tom's aesthetic is inspired by this kind of urban, critical placemaking—where young people claim a space in the city through style and youth culture.

Tom's design proposal for *đây/đó (here/there)* encapsulated this playful and youthful energy. The work, titled *Ngủ Nghê*, was a play on words and a concept that drew on both the phrase *ngủ nghê*, "to sleep," and a mythical creature, *nghê*, that is part lion, part dog. The concept included streetwear with theatrical elements featuring the mythical *nghê* and emphasized the idea of having fun and not growing up (Vietnam Design Week 2021). He teamed up with two mentors, James Bartle of Outland Denim and Vũ Thảo of Kilomet109, who provided guidance and support throughout the project. Thảo was particularly valuable, as she was already familiar with Tom's work and had previously acted as a mentor for him on a previous project. Their established relationship, which was friendly, close, and professional, allowed Thảo to provide tailored advice that complemented James's guidance. James's denim label Outland Denim, meanwhile, brings together a commercial business model with strong sustainability and ethical goals, including "a vertically integrated factory" focused on minimizing environmental waste and an employment focus on supporting survivors of human trafficking with well-paid work and good working conditions (Outland Denim 2023). Both Thảo and James were able to bring their own experience in sustainability and fashion marketing to Tom's work.

Tom's approach to sustainable fashion is particularly noteworthy. He challenges the future of Vietnamese fashion by using donated and upcycled material from the textile factories of Saigon to create capsule collections that reflect the colorful and vibrant image of the city and its people. In doing so, he intertwines representations of Vietnamese heritage and everyday cultures to reflect "Saigonese" qualities, while also upholding traditional Vietnamese values. Tom has been very successful in building a strong, local audience for his work. His social media and brand following since the

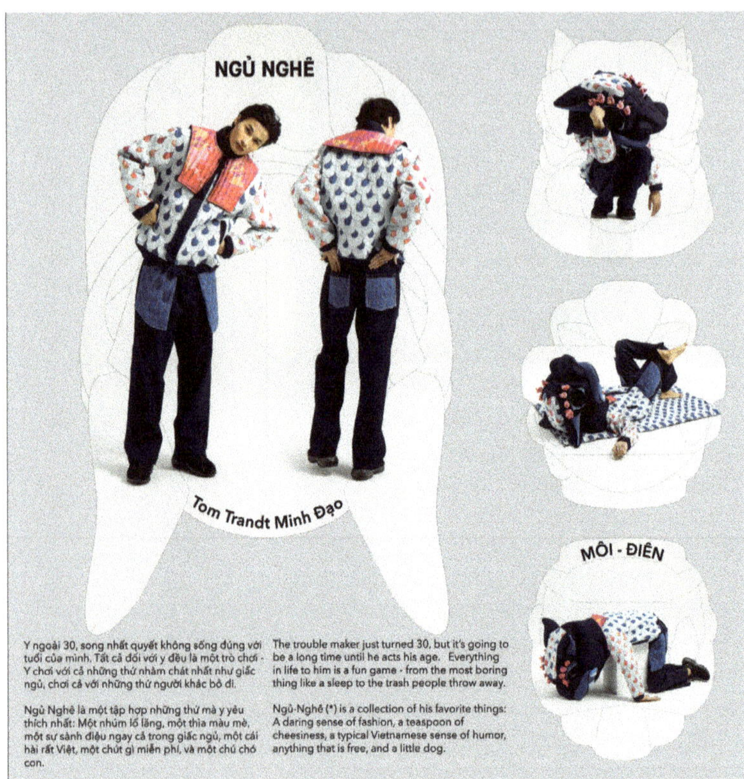

Figure 2.11. Tom Trandt Minh Đạo's design entry for Vietnam Design Week 2021. Image Vietnam Design Week 2021.

opening of his studio underscores the value of this innovative approach to design in the present moment in Vietnam. His work demonstrates the potential for creativity to drive sustainable fashion practices in Vietnam and beyond, providing an alternative to the fast-fashion industry and responding to the country's economic boom in consumerism. He achieves this through limited-edition collections and a modern twist on traditional values voiced through textiles and fabric manipulation to show urban heritage, making a commentary on Vietnamese culture and characteristics through a playful and humorous lens.

Tom's multilingualism facilitated easy communication with his Australian mentor James and the research team. Additionally, Tom's background experience in fashion and textiles provided him with a solid industry knowledge base, which meant that James could focus his guidance on knowledge and experience in the international market, particularly in maintaining quality assurance and production for a larger market—rather than on the nuts and bolts of the design and production of Tom's work. This was also, in part, a result of the online nature of Tom's and James's exchanges—where Tom was able to show great visuals of the work, but James was not able to see and handle the textiles and fashion development firsthand. Thảo's expertise in textile design and production, especially in the Vietnamese context—became significant in this context, where she was able to support Tom in navigating the challenges of designing garments with heavily manipulated fabric and embellishment. Like James, she recognized the importance of maintaining quality assurance in the manufacturing and production process. Thảo's insights and support helped ensure that Tom's designs considered technical standards regarding durability and longevity.

During the mentorship, Tom developed a new line of work, Quấn, that foregrounded his focus on sustainability and Vietnamese street life. This capsule collection was inspired by the proliferation of electrical wires and cables (*quấn* translates to "coil" or "wire" in English) in Saigon streets and the chaotic aesthetic that they represent. It also foregrounded Môi Điên's use of upcycled textiles with a focus on the reuse of long strips of

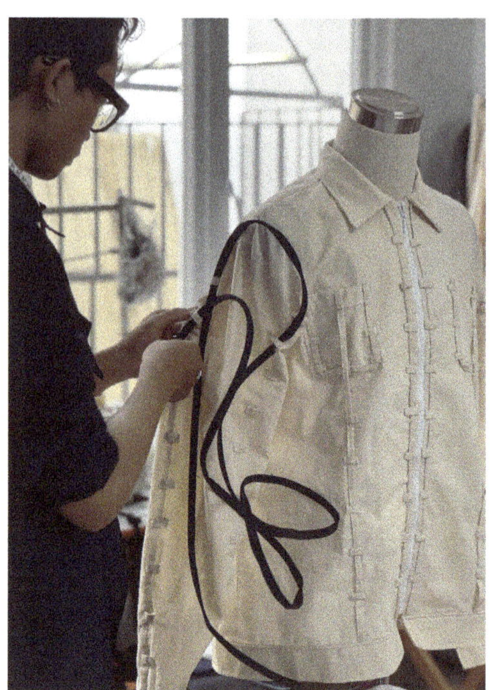

Figure 2.12. Môi Điên team in the studio working on the capsule collection Quấn, featuring upcycled textiles. Courtesy of Tom Trandt Minh Đạo.

fabric—in the style of electrical cables. Tom worked with his studio and a network of local, independent sewers with whom he collaborated closely to create large lengths of fabric composed of a patchwork of these upcycled strips of fabric. His feature pieces included a leather motorcycle jacket and matching pants that were adorned with wild strips of leather (or cables). These items were less wearable and more sculptural—speaking to a particular interest of Tom to push the artistic dimensions of fashion design.

His approach with Quấn advocated for fashion design that costs more and is more artisanal in process than can be seen in lower-cost, mass-produced fashion items. This represented a challenge to dominant commercial approaches to fashion in Vietnam—and an opportunity that came through Tom's participation in *đây/đó (here/there)*, as the mentorship enabled a switch out of "business as usual" for him and an opportunity to experiment. He noted, "This project is important to me because after a few years of working in fashion I think the work itself needs some push in terms of experimentation. We want to go out of our comfort zone, which is the products that are below, let's say 2 million Vietnamese dong [approx. US$80]. And we want to try ourselves with products that cost more and that require more work and more creativity. So this project allows us to do that" (*đây/đó: here/there* 2023).

It is important to note here that Tom's new work foregrounded craft in the "slow making" of painstakingly upcycling long strips of fabric into new materials. This slower approach to fashion speaks to the idea that sustainability in fashion requires different ways of thinking, working, and being—beyond the obvious choices of materials or processes. Tom's approach was

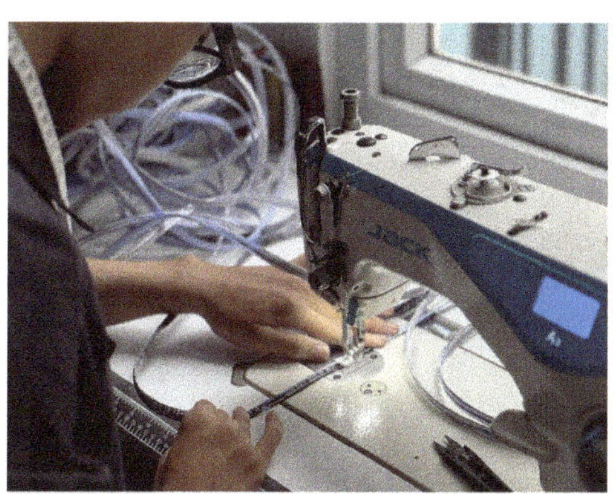

Figure 2.13. Close-up of Môi Điên team working on a strip of upcycled fabric. Courtesy of Tom Trandt Minh Đạo.

highly experimental—testing new ideas and ways of working—and not without its own challenges. The method of upcycling used in Quấn, for example, is very hard to scale up, requires intensive labor, and is costly. Lower-scale production, in turn, requires the use of independent contractors rather than factory workers, which also impacts cost and quality assurance. This brings us back to our argument that creatives like Tom are enacting sustainability as "work in progress" rather than a resolved ideal. In Tom's case, sustainability was a design prompt and creative provocation, rather than a design constraint. Apart from the sustainability aspect of textile upcycling, for example, upcycling as method was of interest to Tom "because the textile supply in Vietnam [specifically] is very limited, so we found all the ways that we can to make ourselves different and one of them is by using very adventurous textile treatments" (*đây/đó: here/there* 2023).

Tom's approach to design, which is both craft focused and artistic, meant other practical challenges, including impromptu modifications to designs, last-minute changes to the collection, and a sense of both creativity and unpredictability. While this challenged the mentors, in some ways it also inspired them. As James Bartle explained, "I think he is quite unique in the way he thinks about his designs and where he wants to see his own brand and career go. What I've taken away is watching how much joy he seems to get from that and working through that process and again taking it into his business" (*đây/đó: here/there* 2023). Meanwhile, Thảo explained, "Through this project with Tom, I also see his strong skill for business. He has clear strategy and the ambition to be able to create a brand to conquer the highly competitive international market. Tom's Môi Điên is a perfect example of the youth of [the] Vietnam creative scene today—socially responsible and fearless" (*đây/đó: here/there* 2023).

Conclusion

Linh's and Tom's work, while different in aesthetic and process, both point to the role that craft has in contemporary fashion markets—what might be considered craft futurism. Both also demonstrate the interconnection of past and future and the idea of sustainability as adaptation. While there is great potential for both practices to develop further in terms of their longer-term aesthetic vision and market viability, the practices of Linh and Tom point to the importance of small-scale, slow-paced, and local approaches to sustainability and creative practice. While these approaches meet a daunting challenge in light of the mass-scale issues of waste and exploitation in the wider fashion industry, they offer up models to challenge hierarchies of creativity and value in these systems. They also point to new ways of thinking about craft's role in contemporary culture. This is an important moment in the context of Vietnam's fashion industry, for example, where there is a strong history of making things and an emergent focus on design. Both Tom and Linh are demonstrating ways to enrich the value chain of sustainable fashion. They are doing this by privileging the making process, centering local values and culture (as opposed to the rampant cultural appropriation of the global

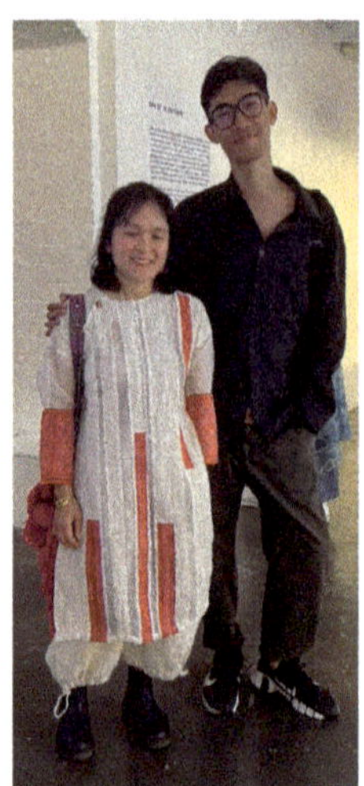

Figure 2.14. Phạm Phan Hoàng Linh and Tom Trandt Minh Đạo at their pop-up exhibition for Melbourne Fashion Week 2023. Courtesy of Becky Lu.

fashion system), and celebrating the potential of local craft—beyond craft cliches.

The case studies of Linh and Tom presented in this chapter reaffirm the need to understand sustainability as a set of practices shaped by cultural and institutional contexts. Cross-cultural collaboration, in the context of *đây/đó (here/there)*, has enabled new understandings of sustainable creative practice, both for creatives like Linh and Tom and for those involved as mentors and researchers, including Dewi Cooke, Vũ Thảo, James Bartle, and the coauthors of this book. In this chapter, we have discussed their work from within the local contexts of Vietnam, while also unpacking how we came to know this work through a transcultural mentoring process. In chapter 4, we circle back to discuss Linh's and Tom's case studies in relation to the idea of mobility—by reflecting on a creative residency that both designers undertook in Naarm/Melbourne in 2023 as an extension of the cross-cultural collaboration.

References

Anh, Phan. 2021. "Vietnam Top Innovator Among Lower Middle-Income Economies: Report." *VNExpress International*. Accessed June 5, 2021. https://e.vnexpress.net/news/news/vietnam-top-innovator-among-lower-middle-income-economies-report-4359937.html.

Angelini, Luciana G., and Silvia Tavarini. 2013. "Ramie [Boehmeria nivea (L.) Gaud.] as a Potential New Fibre Crop for the Mediterranean Region: Growth, Crop Yield and Fibre Quality in a Long-Term Field Experiment in Central Italy." *Industrial Crops and Products* 51: 138–44.

Baptist World Aid. 2021. *Ethical Fashion Guide.* Accessed July 12, 2023. https://baptistworldaid.org.au/resources/ethical-fashion-guide/.

D'Arpizio, C., F. Levato, M. Capellini, B. Flammini, P. Luthra, and G. Improta. 2020. "How Brands Can Embrace the Sustainable Fashion Opportunity." Brief. Bain & Company, October 21. https://www.bain.com/insights/how-brands-can-embrace-the-sustainable-fashion-opportunity/.

đây/đó: here/there. 2023. Accessed December 27, 2023. https://here-there.au/about.

Fletcher, K. 2016. *Craft of Use: Post-Growth Fashion.* Routledge.

Gwilt, A. 2013. "What Prevents People Repairing Clothes? An Investigation Into Community-Based Approaches to Sustainable Product Service Systems for Clothing Repair." *Making Futures Journal* 3. https://makingfutures-journal.org.uk/index.php/mfj/article/view/126.

Hall, C. 2021. "Vietnam Overtakes Bangladesh in Garment Exports." *Business of Fashion,* August 2. https://www.businessoffashion.com/news/global-markets/vietnam-overtakes-bangladesh-in-garment-exports.

Khan, R. 2021. "Relocating Sustainable Fashion: Intercultural Reciprocity in "More than Local" Fashion-Making." *Continuum* 35 (6): 838–52.

Nguyen, H. V., D. Lee, and C. Warren. 2023. "A Comparison of Stakeholder Perspectives of Tourism Development in Sapa, Vietnam." *Tourism and Hospitality Research* 23 (1): 17–29.

Outland Denim. 2023. "About Us." Accessed November 20, 2023. https://www.outlanddenim.com.au/pages/our-story.

Payne, A. 2019. "Fashion Futuring in the Anthropocene: Sustainable Fashion as "Taming" and "Rewilding." *Fashion Theory* 23 (1): 5–23.

Shendruk, A. 2022. "Quartz Investigation: H&M Showed Bogus Environmental Scores for Its Clothing." *Quartz*, June 29. https://qz.com/2180075/hm-showed-bogus-environmental-higg-index-scores-for-its-clothing.

Tran, A. 2012. "Vietnamese Textile and Garment Industry in the Global Supply Chain: State Strategies and Workers' Responses." *Institutions and Economies* 4 (3): 123–50.

Tung, Mai Van., Le Thi Thanh Thuy, and Le Duy The. 2023. "An Introduction to the History and Culture of the Dao People in Thanh Hoa Province." *Hong Duc University Journal of Science* 8 (13): 48–55.

UN Vietnam. 2013. "UN Viet Nam Brief on Young People 2012–2016." Accessed December 29, 2023. https://vietnam.unfpa.org/sites/default/files/pub-pdf/Final%20UN%20Brief%20on%20Young%20People.pdf.

Vietnam Design Week. 2020. "Reo." Accessed November 10, 2023. https://vietnamdesignweek.com/2020/submission/reo/.

Vietnam Design Week. 2021. "Ngủ Nghê." Accessed November 10, 2023. https://vietnamdesignweek.com/2021/submission/ngu-nghe/.

INDUSTRY PERSPECTIVE

Dr. Nguyễn Thị Thu Hà

> I didn't think this "thread" would be that long. Everything is like a fate, a new challenge.
>
> —Pham Phan Hoang Linh, Linht Handicraft, *đây/đó (here/there)* participant

Over the past fifty years, the results of policy research programs on culture, heritage, arts, and creativity at the Vietnam National Institute of Culture and Arts have demonstrated that Vietnam possesses rich and diverse cultural resources, abundant creative resources, and a dynamic and enthusiastic creative community. This community values traditional cultural heritage and seeks to incorporate these values into contemporary creations. Supported by a framework of national policies on culture and cultural industries and political commitments from both central and local governments, such as the National Strategy for Cultural Industries Development in Vietnam by 2020, vision for 2030 (approved in 2016), as well as Vietnam National Strategy for Cultural Development to 2030, the cultural and creative industries in Vietnam have undergone significant positive changes. In 2018, these industries contributed 3.68% to the GDP of Vietnam, and the percentage of people engaged in cultural employment was 6.1% in 2019. Additionally, numerous initiatives have emerged to support and promote the young creative community in exploring and utilizing local materials and cultural heritage for their innovative, contemporary, and global designs. These efforts have contributed to the revitalization of traditional crafts and the resurgence of local knowledge in economic and social development and in environmental protection in Vietnam.

In 2021, amid the global challenges of economic, social, and human impact, cultural and creative activities have faced significant negative effects. However, they have also been swiftly recognized and celebrated as a means to enhance people's resilience in times of crisis. These activities have connected individuals in the context of social distancing and have introduced numerous new approaches and opportunities for sustainable development through culture, art, heritage, and creativity. In Vietnam, the cultural and creative industries have encountered a difficult and challenging period; yet, simultaneously, cultural and creative initiatives have unveiled new opportunities and approaches to unite people and exchange resources, thereby bolstering resilience and adaptability.

Thanks to the connection the RMIT Vietnam team made with the framework of the Vietnam Festival of Creativity & Design, VICAS, RMIT University in Melbourne, CAST, RMIT Gallery, and Vietcraft implemented the "Skilled Hands, Shared Culture" project. This project, with its focus on an online exhibition, served as a conversation between Vietnamese and Australian designers, artisans, and artists, introducing a series of cultural values and unique works of art to audiences in both countries, especially in the context of the COVID-19 epidemic.

The partnership between the Vietnam National Institute of Culture and Arts and

RMIT, motivated by this meaningful project, has paved the way for the continuation of activities that uphold the value of the initial project. This expansion of cooperation with more local and international partners aims to achieve long-term and sustainable development goals for the cultural and creative industries of both countries, exemplified by the *đây/đó: here/there* project from 2022 to the present.

As a long-term collaborative project in the field of design and craft between Vietnamese and Australian designers, artists, and artisans, *đây/đó: here/there* aims to promote contemporary design practice while preserving traditional art forms and craft practices in the context of rapid development and the global challenges of sustainable development in Vietnam and Australia. From 2022 until the present, through diverse activities such as mentoring programs, discussions, community engagement, and showcasing events like displays and exhibitions, the project has yielded encouraging results in various aspects, including advocating for policy change, building capacity, promoting cultural trade, fostering multilateral cooperation, and facilitating international cultural exchange.

From an advocacy perspective, the *đây/đó: here/there* project has reinforced and shared the Vietnamese government's approach to pursuing the development of cultural and creative industries based on local cultural forces encompassing crafts, cultural heritage, and local knowledge; aiming to support a culture that serves as both a goal and a driving force of sustainable development; and enhancing the resilience of communities and societies in the face of global challenges by means of culture and creativity.

The project has shown concrete, visible, and convincing results in bridging the gap in professional skills and innovation capacity between traditional artisans and the emerging generation of emerging creative designers through in-depth mentoring and sharing of experience from multidisciplinary experts from Australia and Vietnam. The multi-stakeholder partnership involved in the project reflects the current context of developing cultural and creative industries in Vietnam, addressing the limitations faced by the central government and localities and the need to diversify sources of investment and funding for projects to develop cultural and creative products. Expanding this cooperation regionally and internationally, particularly with Australia, has amplified the effectiveness of multi-stakeholder cooperation and resource diversification in developing the cultural and creative industries.

The emerging generation of young creatives in Vietnam today is in need of more platforms, opportunities to improve capacity and skills, and access to international markets, as well as challenges, as Linh shared, to unlock their creative capacity and contribute to solving national and global sustainable development problems. The outcomes of the *đây/đó: here/there* project have demonstrated an approach that should be multiplied and applied in Vietnam in the coming years for the sustainable development of creative industries such as design, crafts, fashion, and multimedia art.

CHAPTER THREE

Designing Cultural Values: Reviving Craft Traditions Through Contemporary Design and Materials

The relationship between design and craft is at the forefront in this chapter, where we consider the work of two emerging Vietnamese designers who share a passion for utilizing contemporary design techniques to celebrate Vietnamese craft and cultural traditions. In both case studies, traditional hierarchies of design are destabilized to foreground the importance of material process and craft histories in developing new work that is relevant culturally while engaging with contemporary audiences. Like Linh and Tom, the artists featured in the case studies in this chapter also embrace the idea of sustainability as multifaceted (cultural, social, economic, and ecological) and as "work in progress."

The development of design as a discipline, and indeed an industry, in dominant global discourses stems from a division between the development of the design "idea" and its making, or "craft." It also stems from the commodification and industrialization of products as a key part of modernity. In parallel, the development of the art and design markets has relied heavily on the idea of the work's aura and a sense of elevated value above and beyond the machinations of daily life, the handmade, and the everyday

(Sealy Lineberry and Held 2013). These developments have resulted in an uneven hierarchy of value, with craft on the outskirts of what is celebrated, shown, written about, and canonized in dominant Western art and design sectors. Beyond these hierarchies and schisms between art, design, and craft, there are also internal hierarchies within design, which often position architecture at the top and manufacture/craft at the bottom (Kaufmann-Buhler et al. 2019). Despite this, the enduring importance and popularity of craft as a cultural practice and its deep connection with the practicalities of both artmaking and design demonstrate that this hierarchy is not only elitist but can also be seen as a direct by-product of late capitalism (Jaff 2014). Recent discourses in craft have challenged these divisions, with growing awareness of the political, social, and cultural importance of craft practice—both in and of itself and in relation to contemporary art and design (Cooke 2022; Stupples and Venis 2017). This chapter contributes to this discourse, centering the perspective of creatives in Vietnam.

Turning our gaze away from the dominant narratives of the Northern Hemisphere is useful here in understanding the interconnections of art, craft, and design in cultural life. Vietnamese creatives exemplify this democratization of the disciplines, and emerging Vietnamese designers are demonstrating a strong commitment to upholding, supporting, and celebrating long-held craft traditions in Vietnam—as part of a contemporary design movement and in line with what we are referring to as craft futurism in this book. This is the focus of the work of Lưu Như Ngọc and Đàm Nhã Hân, whose two different practices share a strong commitment to preserving Vietnamese craft and design heritage through contemporary practice. This chapter will examine both of their practices before considering how their shared interests in cultural heritage within contemporary design can inform broader debates around the role of craft and design in sustainable development.

Khứ Hồi (Round Trip)

Lưu Như Ngọc is a recent industrial design graduate from Saigon. Ngọc's proposal was titled *Khứ Hồi*, which means "round trip" or "return journey" (Vietnam Design Week 2021a). Ngọc worked with her team of mentors, Tammy Wong Hulbert and Jennifer Conroy-Smith from RMIT Naarm/Melbourne and Lê Bá Ngọc from Vietcraft in Hanoi, over a period of six months, meeting with them online each month between May and November 2022. Jennifer is an RMIT lecturer of ceramics and an experienced artist. Tammy is an artist and a curator, trained as a ceramics major, lecturing in curating, with a focus on Asian and Asian Australian artists. Ngọc's Vietnamese mentor, Lê Bá Ngọc, is a significant cultural industry figure in Vietnam, promoting art, craft, and design practices from Vietnam and forging opportunities for export, trade, and cultural recognition.

Ngọc's considered proposal focused on how the ceramic waste of the well-known Bát Tràng ceramics village could be reused as material to create sustainable contemporary design pieces. In particular, Ngọc proposed creating a souvenir "wall hanging" to represent the scholarly values of the Confucian Temple of Literature in Hanoi, a sacred site many young people in Vietnam engage in to support their academic journey. The Temple of Literature honors the teachings of the philosopher Confucius (551–479 BCE), which spread from China, and many other important scholars in Vietnamese history. Confucian teachings focused on cultivating personal values—benevolence (kindness and well meaning); honesty; trustworthiness; love and respect for one's parents, elders, and ancestors (filial piety); respect for learning and scholarly knowledge; and loyalty to the state—in order to contribute to greater society. Ngọc's design process reflected her core values of respecting this cultural history while also addressing issues of sustainability via the repurposing of ceramic waste from Bát Tràng ceramics village.

The proposal for *Khứ Hồi* demonstrated originality in considering how ancient traditions continue to be embedded in contemporary Vietnamese culture. Ngọc considered how the practice of honoring Confucian teachings continues for new and emerging generations (Kelley 2006).[4] By taking into consideration the local practices of young people, Ngọc developed this concept based on her observation of and own engagement with these practices.

The purpose of the proposal for *Khứ Hồi* was to develop a series of souvenir ceramic mosaic "wall hangings" designed for the Temple of Literature to represent her interest in "awakening to tradition." The wall hangings focused on the use of nonrecyclable materials; in particular, the reuse of pottery shards, production waste from the

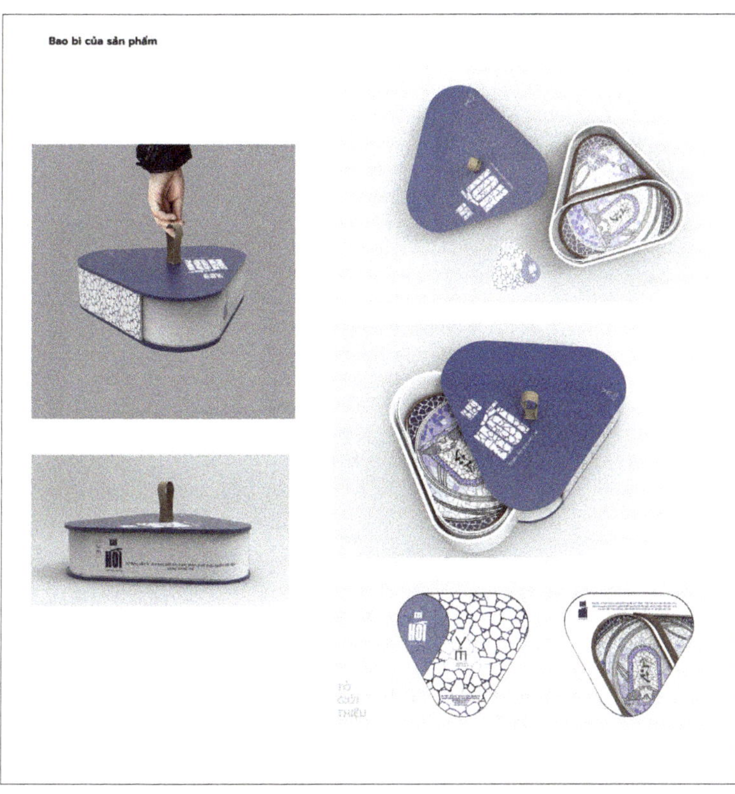

Figure 3.1. A detail of Lưu Như Ngọc's proposal, *Khứ Hồi*, for Vietnam Design Week 2021. Image Vietnam Design Week 2021.

well-known Bát Tràng pottery village. The village is located between Thang Long and Pho Hien, two ancient centers of trade in the north of Vietnam. It is a clay-rich area by the side of the Red River and is one of the most well-known ceramics villages with a history of more than 700 years of production. Bát Tràng ceramics are not only known in the domestic market but were also traded internationally for many generations. Leading up to Doi Moi (the 1986 Vietnamese economic reforms), there was a decline in the export of Bát Tràng ceramics. This decline led to a renewed national interest and reinvestment in traditional craft villages, such as the Bát Tràng pottery village, and thus a revival of the craft industry.

Ngọc's proposal not only gave these waste materials a renewed use, but they also connected a new audience to the traditions of the Bát Tràng pottery village, with its long history of production (Vietcraft 2023). The design concept was a two-way street of the past and the present, featuring two central motifs: the lotus flower (representing divine perfection) and tortoise stele (the tortoise representing wisdom and longevity), a commonly recurring theme at the Temple of Literature. Ngọc's proposal aimed to contribute to contemporary design culture by creating a product with sustainable fabrication by making use of waste materials, while also reconnecting younger generations to the values of a learning and scholarly culture as promoted by the temple. In particular, the Temple of Literature represents the five virtues of kindness, decorum, uprightness, wisdom, and faithfulness that are emphasized by Confucian teachings. Ngọc proposed that by creating a wall hanging as a souvenir representing these values, Confucian temple visitors would be able to purchase the artwork so they could take home the temple experience while also supporting the temple.

Mentoring from a Distance

The experience of developing the project with our industry partners and the monthly mentoring meetings throughout 2022 opened our eyes to the difference between the craft sectors in Vietnam and Australia. The Australian craft scene is made up of small, bespoke, solo traders who work in relative isolation. The only national organization for crafts in Australia is the World Crafts Council Australia, which focuses on overcoming the isolation of craft professionals by connecting the community via dialogue, education, publications, and exhibitions (World Crafts Council Australia 2023). Each state also has its own craft council organization, a representative body that supports these objectives of connecting traders and practitioners in the sector while also educating the broader public about the crafts. The crafts are considered a small sector, not an industry with economic impact. The status of craft is quite different in Vietnam, where craft is positioned as an important industry that contributes to the economy—embodied in the vast number of craft villages across the country, where craft practitioners work as communities more so than as individuals. During this project, we worked closely with our peer mentor Lê Bá Ngọc of Vietcraft, the Vietnam Handicraft Exporters Association. Vietcraft is a peak body organization that supports and promotes handicraft, home decor, home textiles, and gifts. In their representation of the sector, they often host large industry trade fairs, such as Lifestyle Vietnam, promoting hundreds of craft-oriented companies with an emphasis on the fashion and domestic and interior design aspects of the sector.

The team met with Ngọc online each month to realize her design as a pilot project. Through discussions, we developed an achievable timeline. This involved focusing on material testing through to developing finalized pieces suitable for exhibition. We were supported by Bui Thu Uyen, who provided translation through this process. While interpreting did stretch out our conversations, it supported us in being able to communicate effectively. As our cross-cultural mentoring occurred over video meetings, the conditions did pose several challenges. As a graduate of industrial design, Ngọc had limited experience with materials, in particular ceramics. However, her computer design skills were highly developed and her visualization of her project extremely well executed. Without the opportunity for the team to work together in the studio to undertake materials testing, we adapted and explored other methods to demonstrate the potential of working with fired ceramics in various states.

Ngọc spoke about the importance of exploring this gap between her design expertise and the material process of realizing her vision through the mentorship: "First I concentrated on experimenting with the design. Then I researched and learnt how to make the picture—because the original picture was designed by me on the computer and focused a bit too much on details. My mentors advised me to learn about the commerciality of the product and how it can be produced. During this process, I felt that the project was meaningful and I learned a lot from it."

Ngọc began this material experimentation by first testing pieces of Bát Tràng ceramics, which she broke up into shards, before then binding the pieces to a base. She experimented with various types of adhesives and silicon but was not achieving the kind of aesthetic she was hoping for. From here, Ngọc decided to consider firing options. One of the challenges was that Ngọc didn't have access to a ceramic studio and firing facilities where she could use different programs and firing

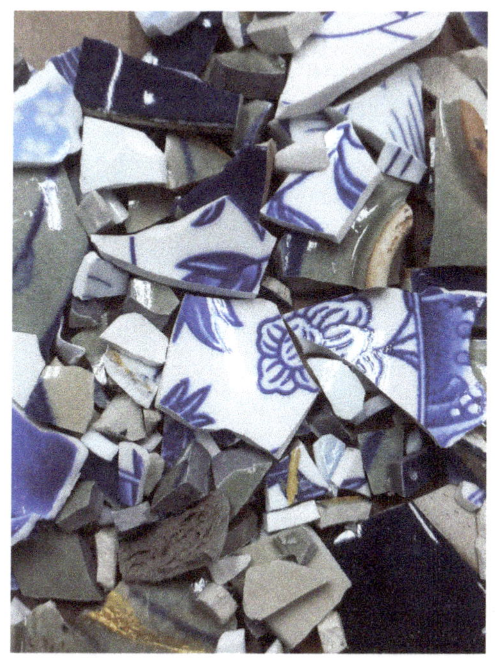

Figure 3.2. Bát Tràng ceramic shards to be used in Ngọc's tests. Courtesy of Lưu Như Ngọc.

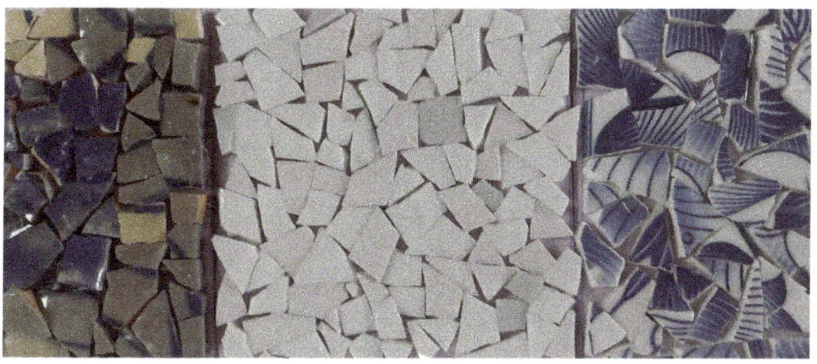

Figure 3.3. The Bát Tràng ceramic shards ordered by glaze colors and patterns. Courtesy of Lưu Như Ngọc.

temperatures. We discussed different clay bodies and firing patterns. We suggested Ngọc get in touch with a local ceramics studio and look at ways in which already fired and glazed ceramic shards could be refired and potentially adhered to a ceramics base. While Ngọc found a local ceramic workshop to collaborate with, there were limited options in changing the firing temperatures—which in turn limited her ability to experiment with the firing process to adhere ceramic shards.

The next experiment Ngọc undertook was using Egyptian paste, a self-glazing clay body that is formed in a mold. Egyptian paste is often used for making beads or small sculptures and, similarly, requires firing. Ngọc sourced all the raw materials and tested the Egyptian paste. While the technique yielded results, the finished product still did not meet her expectations. Ngọc also noted that the cost of materials was quite high, which was an important consideration for developing the pilot. Through these attempts, Ngọc embarked on a great learning curve of understanding the importance of material testing and the time needed to test new materials. As a team, we learned that new material testing was a unique challenge for an industrial design student in Vietnam, where computer design skills are emphasized over extensive material testing—this is quite different in fine arts or craft education in Australia. Due to the proliferation of craft skills and knowledge in Vietnam, moreover, designers often collaborate with artisans to produce their work—as opposed to the more vertical model of design and production found in the Australian craft sector. This material process was of huge benefit to Ngọc, who was able to expand her design thinking and her understanding of the process involved in realizing her design.

Working remotely meant that we had to look for alternative approaches to mentorship without testing ideas in the studio together. It challenged us to think of further solutions. We learned a lot from testing adhering and firing solutions, but at this point we suggested approaching the problem by a different avenue. We began to consider mosaic ware, which is often used in the production of interior and exterior furniture, a slightly larger scale than Ngọc had been working at up to this point. Mosaic ware is also waterproof and hard wearing and has an aesthetic suitable for Ngọc's design. We proposed that Ngọc undertake an internship with a local mosaic company; as a result, Lê Bá Ngọc used his network at Vietcraft to organize an internship with a company specializing in making mosaic outdoor furniture.

Ngọc spent five days with the mosaic company Như Ngọc in Bình Dương, just north of Saigon. Here, she learned how to prepare molds, lay out ceramic tiles, and prepare and pour cement, following how they manufacture items such as tabletops. Ngọc was able to replicate these techniques to a scale that was suitable for her design. We encouraged Ngọc to document what she learned during this process to be able to demonstrate the steep learning curve she had overcome. After learning new skills from industry experts through the internship, Ngọc felt confident to return to her own studio and attempt to replicate these processes within her own designs.

Following the internship, Ngọc replicated these processes in her own studio. She focused on using blue and white Bát Tràng ceramic shards that she broke into pieces to then create the design. She built molds in the shape of her designs and began to lay out the ceramic shards in patterns that emulated her digital illustration. Through the technique

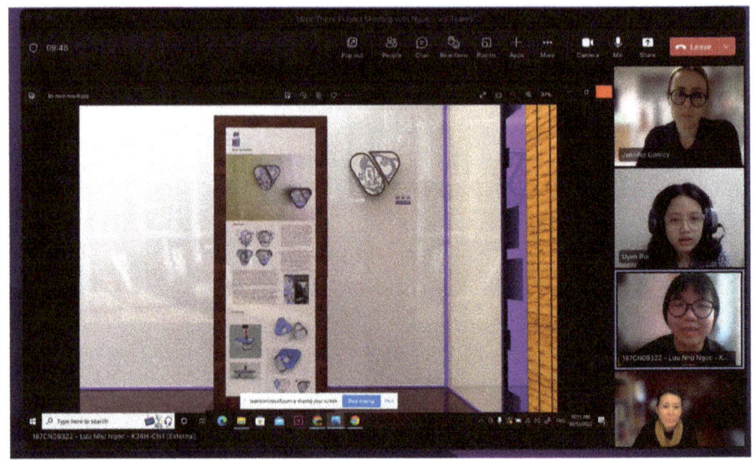

Figure 3.4. Screenshot of one of our final mentoring session with Lưu Như Ngọc. Here, Ngọc is showing us the layout for her exhibition display for the Vietnam Festival of Creativity & Design exhibition 2022.

of mosaic, Ngọc had more control over the aesthetics of the pilot piece. The result looked more like her digital designs, and the processes were quite straightforward.

Once the pilot pieces were ready, the resolved work and process documentation were exhibited as part of the Vietnam Festival of Creativity & Design 2022 in Saigon. Exhibiting the pilot mosaic work and design process provided an opportunity to engage with audiences and demystify the conceptualization and creative processes involved in developing a product.

Returning to the Beginning: *Khứ Hồi*

In reflecting upon this cross-cultural mentorship under the circumstances of global pandemic conditions, working with mosaic company Như Ngọc—as a local Vietnamese industry partner—was a valuable experience for Ngọc's learning. The internship experience gave Ngọc further support in her understanding of working with materials and the confidence to work independently. As we

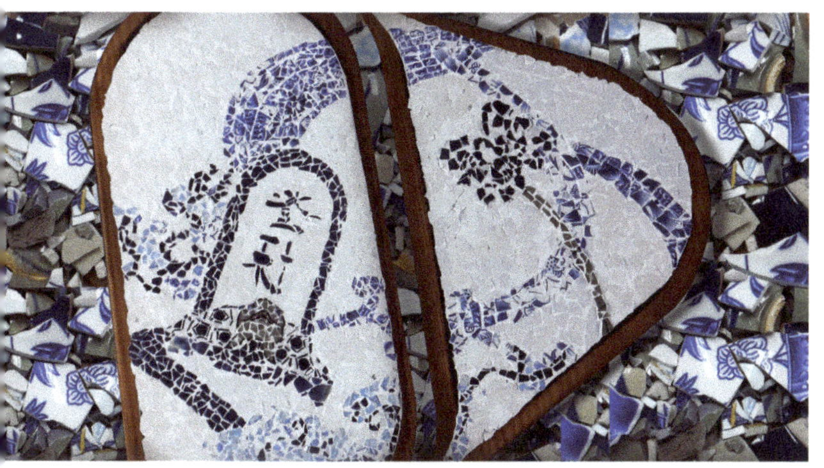

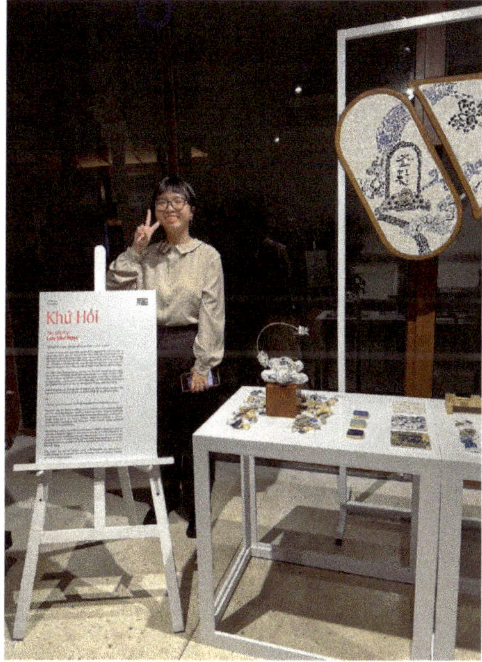

Figure 3.5. Lưu Như Ngọc's pilot piece after her internship with the Như Ngọc mosaic company in Bình Dương.

Figure 3.6. Lưu Như Ngọc's display at the Vietnam Festival of Creativity & Design exhibition in 2022, featuring final work alongside material tests, design concept, and plan. Courtesy of Becky Lu.

enter an era that is heavily reliant on digital design processes, our experience in this project highlights the importance of working with and knowing the nature of materials as a critical part of craft and design practice. Understanding how to work directly with materials cannot be completely replaced by technological automation, although processes may be supported by new technologies. Ngọc's approach is useful here in bringing together her strong computer design skills with these material processes—all while maintaining a deep respect for making traditions. As Ngọc explained, "I learned many things from this project which helped me find the values in my design, and to bring the values to the community. To me, the design with respect to traditional elements are a path for my design career" (*đây/đó: here/there* 2023).

As mentors, we were also given the opportunity to reflect upon the diversity of cultural influences in Vietnam and the ongoing impact of those influences for young people in society. Working with Ngọc, for example, exemplified the ways in which young people have respect for scholarly cultural knowledge, which is deeply embedded in Vietnamese culture. Ngọc's contemporary and sustainable design demonstrated her ability to understand both the aesthetics and interests of younger audiences in Vietnam, while also emphasizing connection to the virtues of kindness, decorum, uprightness, wisdom, and faithfulness as represented by the Confucian Temple of Literature. Importantly, she was able to connect these traditional values with contemporary design aesthetics and approaches. As mentor

Jennifer Conroy-Smith articulates, "Ngọc gives real thought to connecting the traditional elements of culture into contemporary practice and in repurposing to find a new product and a new outcome" (*đây/đó: here/there* 2023).

Nhà (Home)

We now turn to the work of emerging Vietnamese industrial designer Đàm Nhã Hân. In many ways, Hân shares Ngọc's interest in highlighting and celebrating Vietnamese cultural traditions through design. Her approach, however, moves away from the handmade and toward a more stylized, contemporary approach to interior furniture. Hân's work for the *đây/đó (here/there)* project centered around a design for a sleek, geometric TV cabinet prominently featuring indigo dye as an aesthetic device linking it to Vietnamese craft traditions. As a recent design graduate, Hân had sophisticated visual design and illustration skills but had yet to translate them into a built form. The focus of her mentorship and collaboration was on the making process; collaborating with local industry to build and manufacture the work and, in particular, testing out techniques for applying indigo pigment to furniture. She was mentored by the managing editor of *Elle Decoration Vietnam*, Nguyễn Phan Thuỳ Dương; an Australian designer and researcher, Ronnie Lacham (RMIT University); and an Australian designer and the cofounder of furniture and object brand Dowel Jones, Dale Hardiman.

The work was titled *Nhà*, which means home in Vietnamese, and was proposed as

CHI TIẾT SẢN PHẨM/ PRODUCT DETAILS

- Chi tiết sản phẩm được thể hiện qua những đặc trưng cơ bản của nhà 3 gian. Cụ thể:

- Gian ở giữa: Đây là gian chính sử dụng để thờ cúng, được xem là phòng khách của không gian nhà. Gian giữa rộng và khang trang hơn so với 2 gian còn lại ở khu 3 gian.

- Hai gian hai bên nhà ba gian có cửa hẹp hơn ở hai bên cạnh, dùng làm nơi nghỉ ngơi, gồm giường hoặc phản hay sập gỗ. Một gian là phòng dành cho gia chủ. Gian còn lại dành cho khách.

- Thiết kế theo chiều ngang và sử dụng kết cấu khung gỗ như nhà ở truyền thống kết hợp với vật liệu địa phương.

- Details of the product are shown through the central features of the 3 compartments of Vietnamese architecture.

- The main compartment used for worshipping ancestors, considered the living room of the house space. The space is more spacious than the 2 compartments.

- Two compartments on either side of the house are reserved for sleeping, receiving guests used as a resting place. One room is for the family. The other is for guests.

- Horizontal design and used wooden structures combined with local materials.

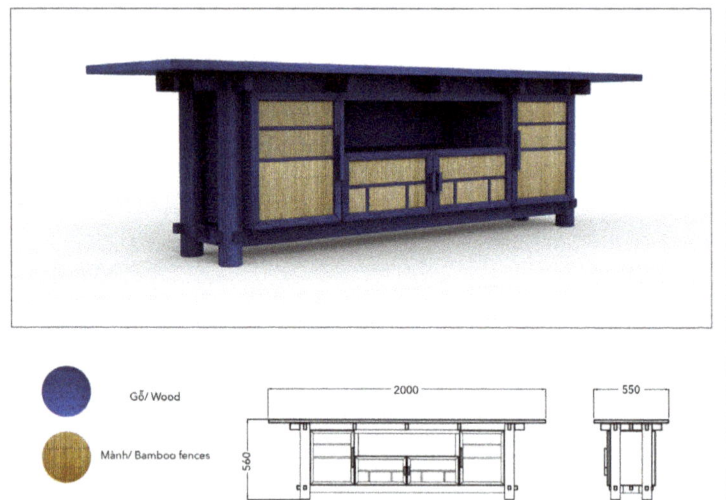

Figure 3.7. Đàm Nhã Hân's proposal, *Nhà*, for Vietnam Design Week 2021. Courtesy of Vietnam Design Week 2021.

a living room TV unit inspired by traditional Vietnamese *ba gian*, or three-room houses (Vietnam Design Week 2021b). This architecture is often seen in traditional villages in the countryside and employs mostly wooden frame structures and local materials (Hartingh and Craven-Smith-Milnes 2007). The design of *Nhà* reflects these houses by compartmentalizing the TV cabinet design the same way the house would be, which is structured around three spaces—*ba gian*—and includes a main space in the middle, usually for worship, along with two compartments on either side for personal rest or

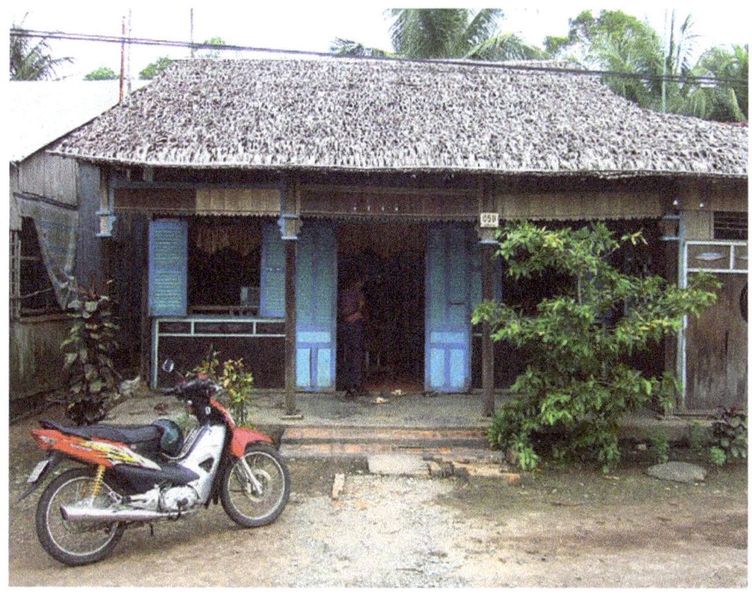

to host guests. As Hân explains, her work "is inspired by the ancient three compartments of Vietnamese architecture and expressed through arrangement by forms, structure, and local materials" (*đây/đó: here/there* 2023). The TV unit mirrors several architectural features of these traditional houses, including, for example, the use of simple local materials (wood, bamboo); vertical struts that mirror vertical columns; thatched cabinet doors that reference the use of thatched screens on the exterior of traditional rural houses; and a sense of connection between inside and outside—a key feature of traditional rural architecture (Ly and Lawson 2018). Hân describes, "The *ba gian* [three-room] house is a very familiar image to the Vietnamese because it is a valuable local asset, and a piece of memory for the soul" (*đây/đó: here/there* 2023). Hân's work is not a simple replication

Figure 3.8. Example of a traditional three-room house from Soc Trang, Mekong Delta, Vietnam. Courtesy of Daniel Berthold, WikiCommons.

of traditional design, however, and instead has a stylized, contemporary aesthetic that is clearly drawing on cultural tradition.

Hân's project was coordinated by Nguyễn Ngọc Thảo, a Vietnamese Australian artist with experience in experimental art forms, including art in public space, as well as a background in fashion. Thảo provided important guidance, particularly in connecting the English-speaking mentors with Hân, fostering a safe space for the collaboration, and working through the complexities of the cross-cultural exchange. Mentorship is an intricate exchange complicated by different identities embodied by the people involved. Gender, ethnicity, and race can influence the effectiveness of mentoring (Mullen and Klimaitis 2021). Creative cross-cultural and cross-gender mentoring can fall into the trap of power dynamics, which favors patriarchal Western values and perspectives. In this case, there were noticeable gaps in verbal communication between mentors and mentees, partly informed by cultural differences, including a commonly held respect for elders central to Vietnamese culture that in Australian culture could easily be misread as "quiet" or "shy." Hân described, however, that her approach was to "observe and learn from the mentor's experiences" (*đây/đó: here/there* 2023). Despite these differences, Hân was able to absorb and apply the learnings from her mentors in her practice, and the collaboration extended and developed her work in ways that would not have been possible otherwise—in particular, through the realization of her design in 3D form. In chapter 4, Thảo reflects on these nuances and, in particular, on how the power dynamics between mentors and mentees influenced the mentorship process.

At the beginning of the project, mentors were strategically selected with considerations of how their expertise might benefit Hân and her design practice and creative journey. With his experience as a design researcher, Ronnie Lacham offered design exercises for Hân to think differently about the initial design. A suggestion to produce a 3D cardboard model of the TV cabinet lifted the annotated renderings on paper to a tangible object taking up space. This gave Hân the opportunity to see what her design looked like in 3D form and to adjust and make changes accordingly. Dale Hardiman, with his experience as the cofounder of the successful furniture and object brand Dowel Jones, offered practical advice on how Hân could extend the design communication of her TV cabinet design so that it would be best placed to attract the attention of global audiences, buyers, and awards. He also gave advice on extending the product line. Dale was particularly interested in learning more about Hân's approach to cultural heritage in her design while introducing her to creative practices from Australia. He explained, "I think it's really exciting to see someone progress so quickly. This is Hân's first piece of furniture and it's really, very good. Once it's presented, not only will it propel her career but liven up her excitement for creative practice in furniture and object design" (*đây/đó*: here/there 2023).

Duong Nguyen from *Elle Decoration Vietnam*, meanwhile, had local insights and was on the ground to assist Hân in resolving the indigo dyeing of the TV cabinet. Having a person with lived experience as a creative

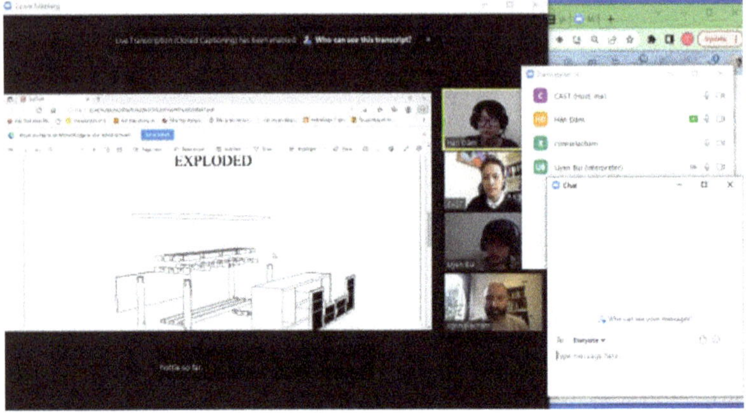

Figure 3.9. Screenshot of mentorship meeting for Đàm Nhã Hân.

practitioner in Vietnam was essential, as these individuals provided insights from an intimate understanding of the local design scene. The indigo dyeing process was one of the more challenging design aspects of the project. The production and application of indigo dye, which has a rich and deep blue color, is an important cultural practice for ethnic minority groups in Vietnam, including the H'mong communities in the Sa Pa region, among others, including the Dao, Nung, and La Chi (Lien et al. 2018). Traditional methods of natural indigo dyeing are typically applied to textiles, and when using natural materials, the process is also sustainable—water by-products can be used, for example, to fertilize crops. This is in contrast to the mass production of synthetic indigo (as found in industrial denim production), which is known to have both sustainability and human health problems. The use of natural indigo pigment was also a way for Hân to think about sustainable design practices. Indigo as a color is ubiquitous with much Vietnamese design, craft, and art aesthetics—and its inclusion in *Nhà*

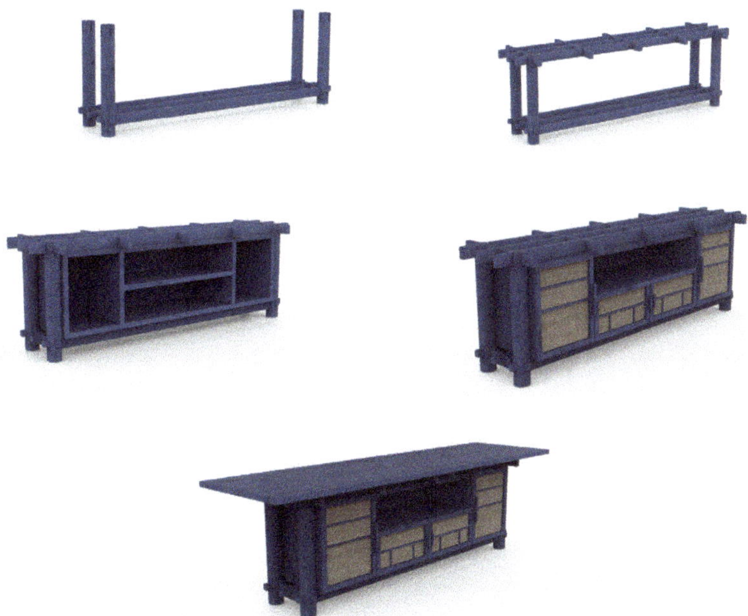

Figure 3.10. Đàm Nhã Hân's technical drawing for the TV cabinet. Courtesy of Đàm Nhã Hâ.

was a significant cultural cue in Hân's design process (Linh 2009). Translating textile-dyeing methods to furniture was always going to be a paradoxical element in the project, so Hân worked with local producers to develop techniques to bring the indigo pigment into a paint form that could be fixed for the final product. The success of this integration of indigo pigment into the final product was one of the more important outcomes of the project and is a testament to the ways in which careful attention to material process, as opposed to focusing on the initial design sketch/plan, can lead to important design outcomes—especially when it comes to considerations of sustainability and/or cultural heritage.

One of the reasons why Hân was chosen for this collaboration was that she demonstrated strong digital design and rendering skills. It was quickly identified that the most appropriate way to support Hân was to encourage her to refine her design and push it to production and into the next step. This was achieved. The collaboration produced a beautiful, carefully crafted finished object, closely resembling that of her original rendering. Additionally, Hân connected with the other emerging Vietnamese designers and presented her TV cabinet design at *CHANGE: Creativity Challenge*, an exhibition and opening event in Saigon for the 2022 Vietnam Festival of Creativity & Design. This opportunity for connection was particularly significant given that the project developed out of COVID-19 lockdowns. This time was particularly hard for emerging creatives, who were trying to forge new networks and find opportunities to show their work, and even more so for students, who were grappling with studying online and without peer networks. Hân explains, "When the project launched the mentorship program, Saigon was under lock down. Just like many other students, or those who move to the city for job opportunities, we couldn't go back home. The image of the house became more familiar and meaningful than ever. That's why I came to this project, I wanted to recreate a sense of the *ba gian* house and its architecture" (*đây/đó: here/there* 2023).

The cross-cultural exchange enabled Hân to also extend her thinking to translate cultural heritage, in this case the traditional architecture of the *ba gian* home, to international audiences. She explains, "In the future, I think for Vietnamese design in general and Vietnamese interior design in

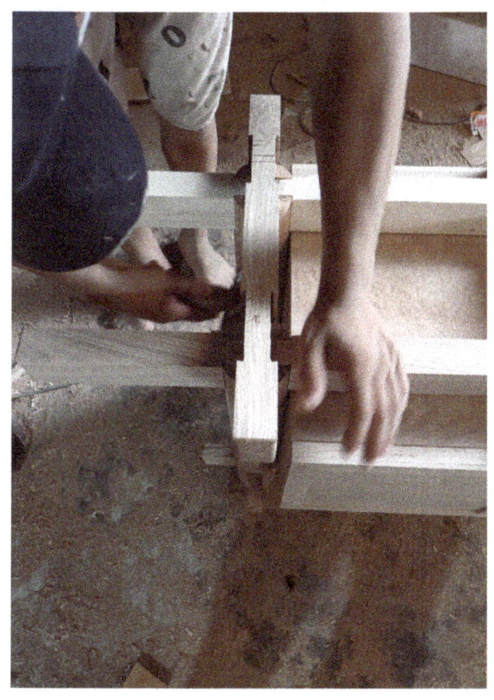

Figure 3.11. Đàm Nhã Hân's cabinet in production. Courtesy of Đàm Nhã Hâ.

particular, design will contribute and become more diverse, meeting the tastes of local and foreign customers" (*đây/đó: here/there* 2023). Importantly, her work also had an impact on her Australian mentors. Reflecting on his participation in the project, Dale Hardiman said, "Each of the four collaborations were touching on such rich cultural heritage—it's really important to see these processes recognized, at a university level, so that it isn't entirely focused on Western design ideals and typologies. Design practice in Vietnam is really alive and so incredibly rich" (*đây/đó: here/there* 2023). This speaks to broader transformations in contemporary design thinking, out of conventionally Eurocentric mindsets focused on aesthetics and markets, toward

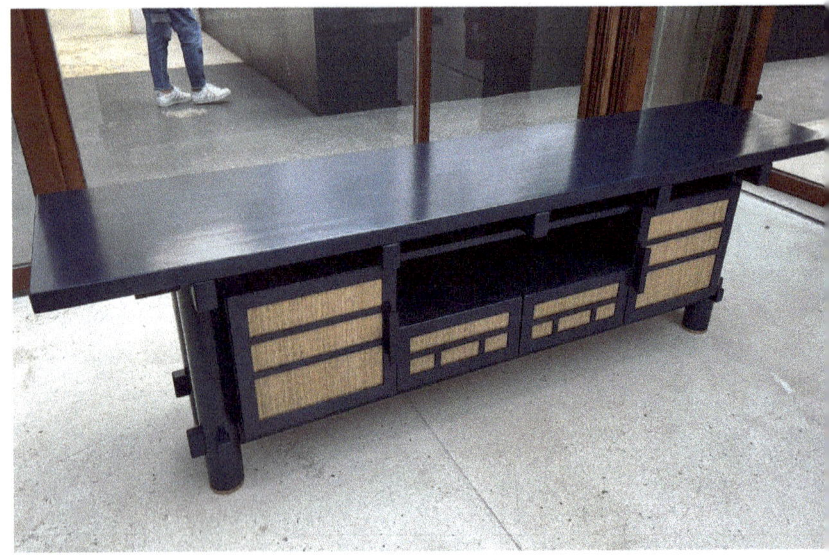

Figure 3.12. Đàm Nhã Hân's final cabinet on display at the Vietnam Festival of Creativity & Design exhibition in 2022. Courtesy of Becky Lu.

reciprocal modes of learning across cultures. In this case, Hân encourages us to learn from Vietnamese design approaches and thinking about tradition, in the form of the *ba gian* architectural home, and sustainability, in the case of indigo dyeing techniques, and at a time of rapid growth and industrialization.

Conclusion

Ngọc and Hân had very different material processes and craft practices, but their case studies are united in many ways—they both foreground important cultural heritage with an eye to contemporary design aesthetics and the interests of the younger generation. They also both faced similar challenges in translating their industrial design skills, with a strong focus on computer-based design techniques, into material form. In both cases, this involved collaboration with local artisans and makers to deepen their understanding of the making process. This, in turn, highlights the strength and vitality of Vietnam's craft industry, where craft skills and knowledge are widely practiced, respected, and valued and form a significant part of the country's economy. As we have demonstrated in this chapter, there are significant opportunities for designers such as Ngọc and Hân to bring together this history of making in Vietnam with contemporary creative cultures in line with the idea of craft futurism.

It is worth reflecting on the extent to which international design education is perpetuating a divide between the practices of "design" and "craft" at a time when craft is being celebrated for its potential creative and cultural counterpoint to the more alienating aspects of the "third industrial revolution." Emerging Vietnamese creative practitioners like Ngọc and Hân embody the potential for craft and design to intersect productively. At the heart of both practices is a strong commitment to upholding, supporting, and celebrating long-held craft traditions in Vietnam as part of a contemporary design movement. They do so in ways that promote the longevity of cultural knowledge, the centrality of craft economies, and ecological sustainable approaches to design thinking. This offers up a holistic approach to sustainability, which as we argue is experimental and adaptive.

References

Cooke, E. S. 2022. *Global Objects: Toward a Connected Art History*. Princeton University Press.

đây/đó: here/there. 2023. Accessed December 27, 2023. https://here-there.au/about.

Hartingh, B. D., and A. Craven-Smith-Milnes. 2007. *Vietnam Style*. Tuttle Publishing.

Jaff, N. 2014. Introduction to *Crafting Creativity and Creating Craft: Craftivism, Art Education, and Contemporary Craft Culture*, edited by Courtney Lee Weida. Brill.

Kaufmann-Buhler, Jennifer, Victoria Rose Pass, and Christopher Wilson, eds. 2019. *Design History Beyond the Canon*. Bloomsbury.

Kelley, L. C. 2006. "'Confucianism' in Vietnam: A State of the Field Essay." *Journal of Vietnamese Studies* 1 (1–2): 314–70.

Lien, Le Thi Hanh Lien, Nguyen Thi Hai Yen, Dao Thi Luu, Phi Thi Thu Hoang, and Nguyen Thuy Linh. 2018. "H'mong Ancient Methods of Indigo Dyeing and Beeswax Batik in Cat CAT Village, Hoang Lien Commune, SAPA Town, Lao Cai Province, Vietnam." *International Journal of Science and Research* 9 (9): 735–42.

Linh, H. T. 2009. "Natural Dyes in Eastern Asia (Vietnam and Neighbouring Countries)." In *Handbook of Natural Colorants*, edited by C. V. Stevens, T. Bechtold, and R. Mussak. Wiley.

Ly, Phuong The, and Gillian M. Lawson. 2018. "Identifying a Language of Space in Pre-Reform Vietnamese Housing." *Journal of Housing and the Built Environment* 34 (1): 111–31.

Sealy Lineberry, H., and P. Held. 2013. *Crafting a Continuum: Rethinking Contemporary Craft*. University of North Carolina Press.

Stupples, Peter, and Jane Venis. 2017. *Art and Design: History, Theory, Practice*. Cambridge Scholars Publishing.

Vietcraft. 2023. "The Art of Ceramics in Vietnam." Accessed November 24, 2023. https://vietcraft.org.vn/mdl/content/action/newsdetail/newsid/119.

Vietnam Design Week. 2021a. "Khứ Hồi." Accessed November 10, 2023. https://vietnamdesignweek.com/2021/submission/khu-hoi/.

Vietnam Design Week. 2021b. "Nhà." Accessed November 10, 2023. https://vietnamdesignweek.com/2021/submission/nha/.

World Crafts Council Australia. 2023. "About." Accessed November 29, 2023. https://wccaustralia.org.au/about/#:~:text=World%20Crafts%20Council%20%E2%80%93%20Australia%20is,third%20wave'%20national%20craft%20organisation.

CHAPTER FOUR

Reflecting on Cross-Cultural Exchange as a Pathway to Sustainable Practices

In this chapter, we share reflections on the processes, challenges, and opportunities involved in each collaboration before recapping the key findings of the book in relation to issues of contemporary craft discourses, cross-cultural exchange, and sustainable craft and design practices, including future research directions.

In *Decolonizing Methodologies: Research and Indigenous Peoples*, Linda Tuhiwai Smith (2021) asks academic researchers to think practically about how power is enacted in cross-cultural research and, in particular, to think about and address how communities will tangibly benefit from the research. She writes:

> Researchers must go further than simply recognizing personal beliefs and assumptions, and the effect they have when interacting with people. In a cross-cultural context, the questions that need to be asked are ones such as: *Who defined the research problem? For whom is this study worthy and relevant? Who says so? What knowledge will the community gain from this study? What knowledge will the researcher gain from this study? What are some likely positive outcomes from this*

study? What are some possible negative outcomes? How can the negative outcomes be eliminated? To whom is the researcher accountable? What processes are in place to support the research, the researched and the researcher? (226)

While our project has included some collaboration with ethnic minority groups and craft villages in Vietnam and has worked with Indigenous creatives in Australia—particularly in our first online exhibition, *Skilled Hands, Shared Culture*—its main focus has been cross-cultural collaboration between Australian and Vietnamese scholars and creative practitioners. In this case, where we have the meeting of a developed economy that is strongly informed by Eurocentric and colonial logic (Australia) with that of a rapidly developing economy and socialist state with a colonial history (Vietnam), these questions are also pertinent. How can we, as researchers, deemphasize dominant colonial ways of knowing and being and learn from our colleagues in Vietnam, a country that has longstanding but underrecognized cultural and creative practices, including a very strong craft industry and culture? How do we navigate the differences in language and cultural biases that we bring to the project? How do we acknowledge the different levels of economic development in each country? How do we ensure that we, as researchers, are accountable?

The first part of this chapter provides a reflective space in which we address some of these questions. To privilege the polyvocal and intercultural nature of the project, we bring forth different voices of our research team, mentors, and mentees, who reflect in their own voices on the opportunities, challenges, and possibilities this cross-cultural project has provided. We do not shy away from the problems and moments when we fall short. In this section, we reflect on the mentorships as *process*, while also recounting some of the public outcomes and events that arose from the project. In particular, we consider how these in-person experiences shifted the dynamics of our collaboration. In the final section, we move on to a discussion of the key findings that have emerged from the four case studies presented in the book, including how cross-cultural exchange might inform our understanding of contemporary craft, art, and design pedagogy and discourse; how these varying practices demonstrate an ongoing and adaptive approach to sustainability; and future directions for the research.

Cross-Cultural Mentorship: Power, Language, Communication, and Cultural Awareness

The various case studies that form *đây/đó (here/there)* have raised important questions on the meaning of mentoring. Effective intercultural and cross-cultural mentoring depends upon the ability of those involved to critically engage with their own positions, biases, institutional dynamics, and constraints. It also depends, in large part, on the success of communication across languages and cultures. While interpretation and translation have an important role to play, there are inevitable gaps and misunderstandings when those collaborating do not understand one another's language.

As coauthor Rimi Khan reflects:

> Everyone in the research team had experience with cross-cultural research, but I think we all still underestimated how much of a challenge this would be. It's easy to assume that all you need to do is get a translator and everything will go smoothly. But it's not that simple. For example, having a translator at meetings means communication takes twice as long. Even when a translator was very good, the presence of a translator is a barrier to the free and easy exchange of ideas. We really felt this when Thảo Vũ was present and she could communicate easily with the designers, compared with Australian mentors. With a translator, conversations often took a long time because of translation and unreliable internet. And there's still the potential for miscommunication. Our translator Uyen was fantastic—she was not an expert in fashion or craft but did a great job of translating specialist language (to do with plant fibers or dyeing techniques). She ended up becoming a very important person within the project team. Even so, there was always the possibility of mistranslations or misunderstandings.

In the case of *đây/đó (here/there)*, addressing these gaps and complexities involved constant adaptation and improvement along the way. Communication was most successful when our Vietnamese mentors (Thảo Vũ, Lê Bá Ngọc) were also present and involved in the mentorship and mediation of ideas and where members of our project team (Becky Lu, Nguyễn Ngọc Thảo) spoke both languages—however broken or imperfect. The importance of this collaboration with local speakers and collaborators with cultural knowledge is highlighted in coauthor Becky Lu's reflection on her role as a coordinator and mentor:

> In my role as one of the project coordinators, I believe my unique position has enabled me to have a dual perspective on Vietnamese and Western understandings, proving valuable in navigating the cultural differences between local Vietnamese artisans and designers and their international counterparts. Relationships are of utmost importance in Vietnamese culture, particularly in building connections between local designers and international markets, where cultural mindsets must be considered and reflected upon.
>
> Throughout the duration of this exchange, we have been mindful of the relationship between the two countries, monitoring the progress of each collaboration to avoid cultural appropriation and ensure an equal level of engagement and reciprocation. We have also taken care to manage any areas of cultural sensitivity that could be lost in translation or within the language used to describe and communicate between all parties.
>
> In reflecting on the project exchange, we have identified both successful aspects and areas that require further development and consideration. Due to the COVID-19 pandemic, mentees and mentors were unable to travel, and online video-calling platforms such as

Microsoft Teams and Zoom became our main channels of communication for project coordination, meetings with designers and mentors, and tracking project progression. However, scheduling these meetings and updates across different countries and time zones presented significant challenges, and technical issues and language barriers also posed obstacles.

This raises the importance of face-to-face exchanges, particularly in the context of cross-cultural collaboration and the tactile nature of textiles and fashion development.

The importance of face-to-face contact and relationship building, as Becky raises, is one of the key findings of the *đây/đó (here/there)* project. This was most evident when we had the opportunity to overcome the digital divide of working online during COVID-19 lockdowns and travel restrictions (from early 2020 to mid-2022) and first began to work together in person. Members of the Vietnam team came together in "real life," for example, for a group exhibition for the Vietnam Festival of Creativity & Design, held in Saigon in November 2022. The first time that members of the Australian and Vietnamese team were able to meet in person was in October 2023, when Tom and Linh traveled to Naarm/Melbourne for Melbourne Fashion Week in 2023 for creative residencies supported by RMIT Culture and the Australian embassy in Vietnam.

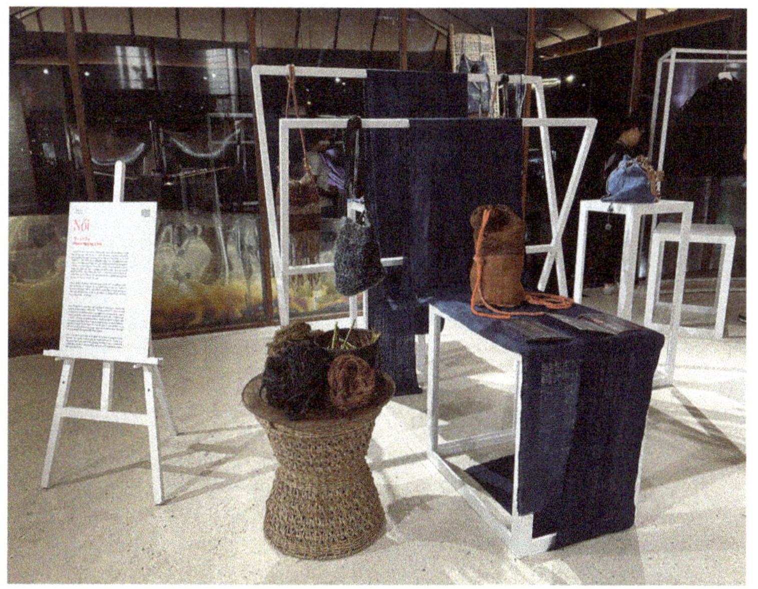

Figure 4.1. *đây/đó (here/there)* exhibition at the Vietnam Festival of Creativity & Design 2022. Detail of Phạm Phan Hoàng Linh's display. Courtesy of Becky Lu.

Mobility, Face-to-Face Encounters, and the "Exchange" in Cultural Exchange

All four of our case study designers—Ngọc, Hân, Linh, and Tom—came together to present their work for the Vietnam Festival of Creativity & Design in November 2022. This was an important outcome of the mentorships and, even more so, a significant moment in the ongoing *đây/đó (here/there)* project, allowing the designers to spend time with members of the Vietnamese team, including our coauthor and fellow project coordinator Becky and industry partners Dr. Nguyễn Thị Thu Hà from VICAS/Vietnam Design Week and Thảo Vũ from Kilomet109. We were struck by the high quality of the finished works presented for the exhibition and, more so, the detailed documentation of the various material, design, and creative processes that each creative undertook as part of the project. This really highlighted for us that the project was grounded in process.

Nevertheless, tensions did emerge in the curation of the exhibition—and this was partly attributable to the ongoing challenges of planning/working remotely in the lead-up to the exhibition. While our online meetings and digital correspondence had gone through the details of the exhibition planning and intentions, there were inevitable gaps in language and communication that only became evident when Ngọc, Hân, Linh, and Tom arrived to help install their work. For example, Linh brought much more textile work and material than could be displayed, while Tom's high creativity meant that his work changed at the last minute and arrived just in time to be displayed before the opening, with mere moments to spare. Having the opportunity to work through these differences in perception and understanding in person was invaluable—and it was through this face-to-face collaboration that deeper relationships were forged among the team. This emphasized the challenges and gaps of working on a creative collaboration through online platforms and, moreover, negotiating varying institutional demands.

While our research team, as individuals, might have come to the project with open minds and a relatively flexible approach, we also had to navigate the expectations of our industry stakeholders and partners. This included the Australian embassy in Vietnam, which had an interest in how the project could support cultural diplomacy, meaning we needed to ensure that there were stories emerging from the project that could be communicated to broad audiences. We also had to support the goals of RMIT in Vietnam and Australia, including research outcomes but also high-quality public presentation of the work via the exhibitions. And our other key partners in Vietnam—VICAS and Vietnam Design Week—had their own expectations in terms of promoting Vietnamese design talent to international audiences. While managing these different stakeholder interests involved compromise, it also opened up new opportunities.

In 2023, the Australian embassy in Vietnam supported travel for Linh and Tom to Naarm/Melbourne to develop their international trade opportunities by connecting with Melbourne Fashion Week. Linh and Tom both have established fashion businesses and creative practices in Vietnam and were therefore considered to be at the right stage for this kind of business development opportunity. The residency involved several different, intersecting parts, including a pop-up exhibition of Linh and Tom's work at RMIT's First Site Gallery in the Naarm/Melbourne central business district; a designer talk for Melbourne Fashion Week; a textile repair workshop with Tom as part of fashion lecturer Georgia McCorkill's Repair Cafe sustainable fashion workshop series; a retail pop-up for Linh at TSS in the adjacent suburb of Collingwood; and finally, a "meet the designer" event that also included a separate book launch of Kerry Nguyen-Long's *Vietnam Visual Arts in History Religion & Culture* (2023).

There was a sense of both excitement and relief when the Naarm/Melbourne team of Thảo, Grace, and Tammy finally met

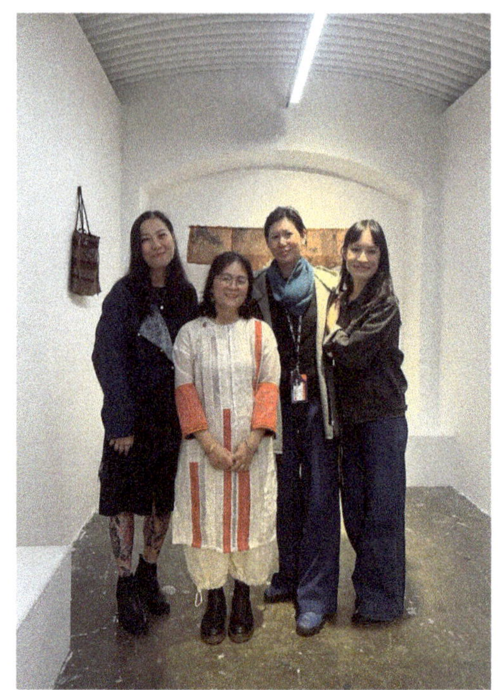

Figure 4.2. Clockwise from left: Becky Lu, Phạm Phan Hoàng Linh, Tammy Wong Hulbert and Nguyễn Ngọc Thảo at the *đây/đó (here/there)* pop-up exhibition at RMIT First Site Gallery, Naarm/Melbourne, Australia, 2023. Courtesy of Becky Lu.

colleagues Becky and Rimi and, of course, Linh and Tom—and when Linh and Tom finally met their mentors. It also shifted the dynamic from the more formal, procedural space of online "meetings" held on business software such as Teams and Zoom toward a more relational and social atmosphere. As Linh's industry mentor Dewi Cooke reflected:

> Meeting Linh in person and being able to finally see and touch her work was wonderful. It is difficult to replace the value of these kinds of interactions. However thanks to the many months of meetings and emails we had built a rapport of sorts, so hosting her in our shop felt very natural. I'm thankful to Rimi for facilitating

our conversations over those months to help keep momentum and energy for the project going, and indebted to our translator, Uyen, for being the conduit which connected us all.

Linh brought with her a good friend and collaborator, Hoang Hong Hanh, who also had a background in fashion. Hanh played an important role in supporting Linh and as a conduit to relationship building. The exhibition became the gathering-point for the residencies. This was where the public talk, repair workshop, "meet the designer," and book launch all took place. It was also the site where the research team came together and worked alongside one another to curate and physically install the exhibition—with support from RMIT Culture's team, led by Erik North. For the Naarm/Melbourne team, this was our first opportunity to physically handle and see the textile works of Linh and Tom and deepened our appreciation of the complexity and creativity of their practices.

These events drew a wide and varied mix of people—from the fashion-forward audiences of Melbourne Fashion Week to local creatives in the contemporary art and craft scene. In particular, we were struck by the number of Vietnamese diaspora attendees at the designer talk. It became clear that the exhibition and events provided a significant and unique forum to unpack the relationship between Vietnam and Australia along with the significance of seeing contemporary expressions of Vietnamese identity in Australia. It was noted that it was important to have a Vietnamese presence in Melbourne Fashion Week—adding to calls for greater cultural diversity in the fashion scene in Naarm/Melbourne. And poignantly, conversations emerged about whether we need to move on from focus on the Vietnam War in understanding the ongoing relationship between Australia and Vietnam.

The benefits of the residency were reciprocal. Just as Linh and Tom's visit made an indelible mark on the local creative community, the travel opened them up to new opportunities and new kinds of value—in particular, by internationalizing and reframing their craft. In many ways, this is where the cross-cultural exchange took place. Linh, for example, learned about the Australian art, craft, and fashion markets. She faced the challenge of applying a local "value" to her pieces in this

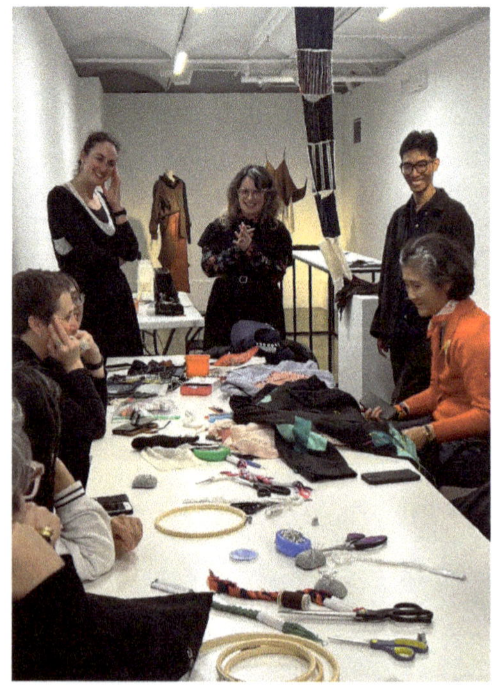

Figure 4.3. Repair Café workshop featuring Tom Trandt Minh Đạo as part of his Naarm/Melbourne residency at RMIT First Site Gallery, 2023. Courtesy of Becky Lu.

market, which was a useful learning opportunity for everyone. How can you place an adequate monetary value on the innumerable hours of handmade labor that went into her processes, where fibers such as ramie are sourced, processed, woven into fabric, dyed, and then finally turned into "products"? Dewi reflected on this tension between valuing Linh's slow craft processes and applying market logic in an Australian context:

> Pham Hoang Linh's textile work is thoughtful, reflective, and attuned to the natural world surrounding her home in the Sa Pa hills of northern Vietnam. The same could be said about Linh herself: a quiet, classically trained artist, she's found a creative outlet there through the making and selling of naturally dyed and handwoven garments and accessories which champion traditional craft methods.
>
> In many ways, this slow, craft-focused approach characterized my own process of mentorship with Linh. Over several months and through patchy video conferences, Linh's plans for her line of Linht Handicraft woven bags was quietly revealed as she brought us into her world of collaboration and experimentation with the weavers and dyers of local hill tribe communities. Although [Linh was soft] spoken, I quickly understood that [she] should not be mistaken for being uncertain: her creative vision and intent was clear.
>
> Once we knew she was coming to Melbourne and The Social Studio would be hosting a pop-up of her work, I was

able to see Linh's pieces through a more commercial lens which, I hope, was useful to her. Price points and most popular products were discussed, although I note that these emails were mostly handled by her friend, Hanh, due to the language barrier.

The experience in Naarm/Melbourne—both the exhibition and the TSS pop-up—helped expose Linh to an international market, in particular a more design- or art-oriented market. This was different from the local market in Vietnam, which for Linh's work has gravitated toward tourist handicraft.

Tom, meanwhile, reached out to local retailers and developed a multistore wholesale strategy for Môi Điên Studio in just a few short days. This was indicative of his eye to the global market and aspirational business approach. In a more practical sense, the travel opened Linh and Tom up to new experiences—good and challenging. As our coauthor Rimi reflected, "Linh and Hanh missed Vietnamese food and Tom hated the cold weather of Melbourne in spring!"

Home: Reflections on Being a Houseguest

As we have argued so far, the subtlety and role of cultural difference is essential in navigating cross-cultural mentorship and collaboration. To delve deeper, we now turn to share a critical reflection from coauthor Thảo about her experience coordinating the mentorship team for emerging designer Đàm Nhã

Hân. In this extract, Thảo points to the ways in which cultural differences can inform how we might perceive the "success" of mentorship and collaboration, along with the challenges of online cross-cultural exchange:

> Since 2021, I was involved in the *đây/đó (here/there)* project as a coordinator. In this experience, I learned to draw on my position as a Vietnamese Australian creative practitioner to help facilitation of understanding between emerging Vietnamese industrial designer Đàm Nhã Hân, managing editor of Elle Decoration Vietnam, Thuy Duong Nguyen Phan, Australian designer and researcher, Ronnie Lacham (RMIT University) and Australian designer and cofounder of furniture and object brand Dowel Jones, Dale Hardiman.
>
> Mentorship is an intricate exchange which is complicated by different identities embodied by the people involved. Gender, ethnicity, and race can influence the effectiveness of mentoring (Mullen and Klimaitis 2021). In this mentorship, the coordinator and the mentors were the guests, and we were invited to temporarily stay in Hân's house. In this reflection, I propose that within cross-cultural mentorship programs, the coordinator and mentors must embody the role of the guest. For the mentee to thrive in this process, the guests must abide by the house rules.
>
> While each mentor played a pivotal role in pushing Hân toward the next step, there were complex obstacles that everyone had to overcome, which were

sometimes unexpected and uncomfortable. It is only with hindsight that I can begin to untangle the complexities of these challenges and offer some suggestions for those interested in initiating and facilitating creative cross-cultural exchanges.

On-Screen and Off-Screen Actions

Hân was based in Vietnam, and the mentors were dispersed across Vietnam and Naarm/Melbourne, Australia. This distance had meant that we all had to meet via Zoom. On-screen, the mentors attempted to build resilience in Hân by challenging the feasibility of her design. These constructive conversations enabled fundamental learning as Hân was pushed to leave her comfort zone. With the assistance of a translator, the communication between the mentor and mentee was adequate. However, the already subtle cultural nuances were easily missed, and it was difficult to build a rapport with limited personal and face-to-face interactions. Hân was somewhat reserved and listened attentively, but did not speak a lot.

Upon reflection, I realize that she was put in an uncomfortable space. Fundamental aspects of Vietnamese culture include showing respect for elders and to speak only when spoken to. Everyone in the room was older than Hân, which contributed to the power dynamic. This significance of this was not registered at the time. With that in mind, the [one-word] responses from Hân [did not indicate disinterest, but] politeness. Additionally, a common trait of Vietnamese people is to be nonconfrontational. Hân was vulnerable, with both her work and attitude under the scrutiny of . . . Western gazes. Even if Hân disagreed with the mentors' comments or directions, she was unlikely to express her discontent [so] as to avoid conflict.

Most of the progress happened off-screen. Between our Zoom meetings, Hân independently researched, sourced, and communicated with local makers who could bring her design to life. What this suggests is that Hân was invested in the project and had listened to the mentors' critiques. Perhaps it was the pressure of having to respond instantly that made Hân appear reserved.

Speaking My Language

Initially, we were unaware that Hân required a translator, which made the first meeting awkward. With my broken Vietnamese, I temporarily stepped into the role of translator and clumsily [facilitated] the communication between Hân and the mentors. In the next meeting, we introduced a translator, Uyen, and Hân was slightly but noticeably more at ease. Even so, the power dynamic was amplified, as English was the predominant language, and everyone except Hân was fluent in it.

To compound the issue, most of the written correspondence to Hân was also in English. One of our partners who was responsible for organizing artists' agreements had sent Hân and the other Vietnamese designers a hefty document written in English to be read, understood, dated, and signed as soon as possible. For a person who doesn't read or write English, this was understandably an intimidating request.

In the beginning, my email exchanges to Hân were also in English, and Hân was unresponsive via email. However, as soon as I translated the emails into Vietnamese, Hân's responses became longer, detailed, and prompt. It is important to acknowledge that while I had translated the emails to Vietnamese, the accuracy and flow of the communication was only as reliable as Google Translate was. Although translating the emails was relatively simple, it took some effort. It dawned on me [then], the additional labor that Hân had to perform before the emails were translated. This original distribution of labor was unseen and represents the invisible work of non-English-speaking collaborators in cross-cultural collaboration where English is prioritized.

There were also some other subtle Vietnamese conventions which I added to our email exchange, including addressing Hân as "em" (younger sister) and signing off as "chị" (older sister). These are terms of endearment, and I believed that it had strengthened the trust that Hân had toward me and, by extension, the *đây/đó (here/there)* team and project. It was also important to me to address Hân by the Vietnamese spelling of her name and to provide her the opportunity to dictate how she would like her name to be presented on the *đây/đó (here/there)* website.

> Nhà is Hân's house. In this project, Hân had invited us in. Not only did she subject her product design for critique, but she also welcomed us into her design process and thinking. Like a host, she trusted us to take care of the space and treat it well. There were times when I had felt a little confused as to why the Zoom meetings were not as productive as I had hoped they would be. I had not realized that I had my own perceptions of what a successful mentorship should be—that is, one with extroverted mentors engaging in energized conversations with an equally extroverted and keen mentee. In the beginning, I had not registered the different obstacles that Hân was facing. However, as soon as I embraced my positioning as a Vietnamese person, I felt a shift in the project. I had to learn the house rules and abide by them. The sudden responsiveness from Hân after I translated my emails and addressed her as em, indicated that Hân was keen to engage. She just needed us to meet her halfway. I was not the perfect houseguest. Hopefully, with these reflections from the *đây/đó (here/there)* project, you can be a better one.

What Thảo articulates so well here is the ways in which cultural misunderstanding can be very implicit, even silent. The work of those involved in creative collaboration across cultures, therefore, is to pay attention to the silences, to the gaps in communication, as much as to notice to the obvious differences in opinion or approach, and, importantly, to ask the question of who has power, who may not, and, ultimately, who is benefiting from the collaboration and partnership.

Hân's reflection on the project, meanwhile, speaks to the professional development opportunity of working with international and local design industry professionals. Given the power dynamics Thảo outlined, Hân was less interested (or perhaps willing) to reflect on the cross-cultural subtleties or challenges of the mentorship and more focused on the practical and material challenges of her creative process: "During this project, I learned how to collaborate effectively with professional consultants and develop design solutions. With the support of the design competition and guidance from overseas mentors, I believe the most successful aspect of the project was the realization of the product. It is not just a concept on paper; it is actively used in daily life."

When she reflected on the challenges of the mentorship, again, her reflections were in relation to the technical process: "Additionally, participating in the competition opened up opportunities for me to work with design industry companies. I did face challenges during the technical phase of the project. Initially, I intended to dye the product indigo, but due to difficulties in testing, I opted for PU paint instead."

It is important to note that Hân's reflections also speak to her deep commitment to contributing to the broader craft and design ecosystem in Vietnam—beyond her individual mentorship. This speaks to a trend among younger creative practitioners in Vietnam to want to contribute to industry growth and transformation: "Being a part of this project has been a great honor for me. It has also provided me with a chance to contribute to the development of the design industry in Vietnam, particularly in fostering the growth of creative products that meet the needs of both domestic and international customers."

Reciprocal Learning and Cultural Exchange

Another key aspect of successful intercultural or cross-cultural mentorship is the recognition that every person involved stands to learn, and benefit from, the knowledge exchange. That is to say, it is important that we move away from a hierarchical exchange in which one culture is presumed to have greater knowledge/expertise to bring to the table. While most people embarking on cross-cultural mentorship and creative exchange would take this reciprocity as a given, we found instances in *đây/đó (here/there)* when implicit or unconscious bias edged into the exchanges. We now turn to Grace McQuilten to reflect on some of these subtle instances:

> The dominant mode of communication in education and industry in Australia is email. At times, institutional partners and stakeholders involved in the project in Australia offered—with a spirit of generosity and care—advice for our Vietnamese mentees and industry partners around standards and expectations of workplace "professionalism." This meant specifically the advice that our Vietnamese partners and designers should reply more promptly to emails or respond to our request to sign an artist

agreement or fill out a detailed pro forma templates providing biographical information and images. What our colleagues in Australia inadvertently missed in providing this advice is that in Vietnam, other forms of communication are preferred over email. For example, sending messages on WhatsApp or Facebook is far more likely to engage partners and elicit responses. Also, the formality of our approaches might feel "professional" in an Australian context, but this doesn't always translate across cultures and instead can be perceived as a barrier to engagement. Why are our processes so tedious, so wordy, so detailed, and time-consuming? Couldn't we get things done more efficiently with a phone call or text? This is not to say that one approach is better than the other—but in order to achieve a mutually beneficial and reciprocal cross-cultural exchange, we need to be open to learning different ways of doing things, and to meet our collaborators at least halfway. My preference would be to go much further than halfway!

One of the best aspects of the collaboration was that mentors did engage genuinely in a learning process, and many spoke about the benefits and learnings that they took from the exchange. Rather than the Australian industry mentors being the "experts" offering "advice," they became participants with as much to gain. Linh's mentor Dewi, for example, talked about the reciprocal learning opportunities she received by being part of the project:

> What I've loved about it is seeing how Linh has embedded herself in a part of her country where some of this knowledge and craftsmanship exists. And I think there is something for me very inspirational about seeing that, about how humble she is in a way to want to create these items and products with other community members because she herself is really taken with the work that they do and there is no real sense of superiority. It's very much that she is learning from them, as we are learning from her.

This reciprocity was also evident in Tammy Wong Hulbert and Jennifer Conroy-Smith's reflection on working with Ngọc:

> We saw this as an excellent opportunity to learn from Ngọc and each other through the process, developing a deeper understanding of the vibrant and expansive craft village scene in Vietnam. Both Jennifer and I had some knowledge of the rich craft village scene but were keen to learn more through working with Ngọc. There are many craft villages in Vietnam that specialize in various types of crafts. These villages form the backbone of Vietnam's creative industries, providing vast employment for small to medium businesses in urban and regional areas. It is a sector that contributes significantly to Vietnam's growing economy.

Tammy and Jennifer also reflected on the importance of adaptation and flexibility in working across cultures and remotely via technology:

The *đây/đó (here/there)* project was also initiated during the global pandemic lockdowns during 2020–2021. Although the mentoring occurred in 2022, when lockdowns had ended in Naarm/Melbourne, our project continued as an online project, as traveling overseas was still challenging throughout this period. One of the legacies of the pandemic period is that it changed our working conditions dramatically in both negative and positive ways. We adapted to working remotely with the support of video technology and we were able to meet with our collaborators more easily. This was fortunate in many ways, as we were able to develop this international project, which meant we could meet with Ngọc regularly to discuss her development, even though we were in different countries. It was also challenging, as there were many instances when we would have benefited from working together in the studio, especially during the early stages of ceramic firing testing. The challenge of physical separation gave us an opportunity to think of alternative ways for Ngọc to still acquire the skills necessary for her project and gave her an opportunity to work with local artisans, including at the mosaic workshop.

In Ngọc's reflection, she spoke about valuing the technical and material opportunities offered by the mentorship—including the practical skills of making and being involved in the full process of product creation. She reflected: "As an introverted and shy person,

I usually take a long time to start exploring new things. However, during this experience, I learned about the process of creating a product. I also gained a deeper understanding of how traditional materials can be used in modern industry to support long-term growth."

Like Hân, Ngọc's reflection was largely positive in terms of the mentorship and collaboration. This potentially speaks to the power dynamics and difficulties faced by mentees in a mentorship to speak up and criticize their collaborators. It also speaks to Hân's and Ngọc's interests in the project. They were focused more on their own creative practice, professional development, and learning journey, along with concerns about craft futures and sustainability in Vietnam's creative industries, than on the nuances of cross-cultural exchange. As Ngọc shares:

> Looking back, I realize that my biggest challenge came from myself. At the time, I was still young, lacking focus and experience in problem-solving. Through this experience, I learned that design is not just a job, but a journey that allows me to grow and expand my potential. Even though I am now a furniture designer, the lessons I learned have helped me improve my design skills. I now approach new topics with greater responsibility, dedication, and a focus on sustainability.

As Vietnam has such a strong and dynamic craft industry, creatives like Ngọc, Hân, Tom, and Linh were all able to collaborate with local artisans and craftspeople as part of their mentorship—particularly where skills gaps were identified. This was something that our Australian mentors were able to appreciate and learn from—from a perspective of a craft culture where the creator is often also the maker, as is widely the case in Australia, the ease of collaboration and collective craft culture in Vietnam offered new ways of thinking about creative practice. This reciprocal learning, moreover, served to challenge established hierarchies of creativity and innovation across both countries. As Rimi noted: "Not only did we find creativity in Vietnam, but we found creativity through exchange and mobility—the project was not just performing for Australian audiences, but foregrounded audiences and markets in Vietnam."

This reflection from Rimi speaks to the importance of doing cross-cultural collaboration well, particularly in the context of the creative industries, where issues of cultural appropriation frequently arise. While there are flourishing discourses around legal frameworks to protect cultural heritage, practice, and knowledge, there are fewer reflections on what productive and positive forms of cultural and creative exchange might look like in practice. As Rimi observes, "This is important to think about given that intercultural encounters are part of life—so how can we build on these encounters to work toward a more equitable creative industry landscape?"

In Ngọc's final reflection, she drew links between her personal experiences in *đây/đó (here/there)* and these broader ambitions to contribute to the creative industry landscape in Vietnam: "When I consider the greatest success of the 'đây/đó' project, I realize that

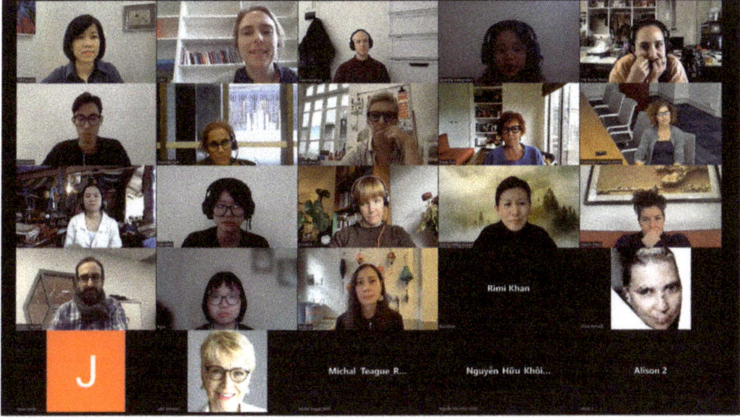

Figure 4.4. Screenshot of *đây/đó (here/there)* project meeting with all stakeholders, artists, and research team.

it wasn't just one factor. Many elements contributed to its success. It came from the dedication of the mentors, the cooperation between different organizations, and the opportunity to gain hands-on experience with local businesses. Most importantly, the commitment and determination of everyone involved—those who worked hard to support cultural exchange, connect communities, and preserve traditional craftsmanship in Vietnam and Australia—made the biggest impact."

Likewise, Linh shares this future-oriented perspective, connecting her learnings with both a desire to share Vietnamese craft values with the world and aspirations for future artists and designers in Vietnam:

> Through the project, I have met and shared my work with people who love arts and crafts, and introduced the cultural values of the Vietnamese people to friends around the world. In addition, I have found new materials for my own creations. The mentors are very enthusiastic in sharing their experiences and

giving their opinions on developing my products from a drawing to the creation of the product. I am very happy to be a part of the project. I hope that in the future, the project can develop further so that young designers like me have the opportunity to learn and interact with the community [of people] who love arts and crafts.

References

Mullen, C. A., and C. C. Klimaitis. 2021. "Defining Mentoring: A Literature Review of Issues, Types, and Applications." *Annals of the New York Academy of Sciences* 1483: 19–35.

Nguyen-Long, Kerry. 2023. *Vietnam Visual Arts in History Religion & Culture*. Thế Giới Publishers.

Smith, L. T. 2021. *Decolonizing Methodologies: Research and Indigenous Peoples*. Bloomsbury Academic & Professional.

Conclusion and Future Directions

In this book we have explored the ways in which cross-cultural exchange can inform and transform contemporary understandings of craft, art, and design pedagogy and practice. The *đây/đó (here/there)* project has enabled us to question and challenge dominant hierarchies that persist in global discourses of art, craft, and design; namely, the unequal binary of fine art over craft in global markets and the similarly problematic binary of design over production/making, with the flow-on effects of exploitative labor conditions and unsustainable practices. Instead, we have attended to the ways in which emerging creatives in Vietnam are centering craft in their creative practices, design thinking, and material processes—in spite of dominant educational models that still maintain structural divisions between "design" and "making" in pedagogy. In turn, the project has enabled us to appreciate and recognize the dynamic craft industries and cultures in Vietnam, and by extension the Asia Pacific—a geographic region often overlooked in contemporary craft discourses. In the context of Vietnam, craft is a means of preserving tradition while at the same time offering opportunities for experimentation and innovation—what we have referred to as "craft futurism."

The book has examined how the different creative practices of our case studies—which include fashion, textiles, furniture design, woodworking, and ceramics—demonstrate adaptive approaches to sustainability—understood in a broad sense to include environmental, economic, social, and cultural dimensions of sustainable practice. The approaches of Ngọc, Hân, Tom, and Linh are experimental and not without challenges. While Ngọc focused on the reuse of ceramic waste from Bát Tràng craft village, the labor involved in painstakingly transforming these fragments into new works poses barriers to scaling up and, by extension, resolving the extent of ceramic waste at the village. While Hân's practice focuses strongly on sustaining the cultural heritage of the *ba gian* house and use of natural, indigo pigment, it was less clear where she sources the raw materials for her furniture and, similarly, at what scale/s the work can be produced. In Tom's practice, meanwhile, there were real challenges in the upcycling of deadstock materials; Linh's practice constantly needs to adapt to varying materials, the local climate, and the learning process of working with local Indigenous groups.

As we have demonstrated, the opportunity for mentoring and cultural exchange—as provided in *đây/đó (here/there)*—has pushed Ngọc, Hân, Tom, and Linh to do more and think more about these questions of sustainable practice and processes. This has included thinking in terms of cultural sustainability (maintaining cultural practice and identity), social sustainability (supporting income streams and livelihoods for communities in Vietnam), and economic sustainability (how to build a business and scale up production), as well as thinking about the significant role of ecological sustainability (circular approaches, minimizing waste) at a time of ecological crisis in the Asian Pacific. Importantly, the creative approaches deployed by Ngọc, Hân, Tom, and Linh emphasize the idea of sustainability as "work in progress"—adaptation and experimentation rather than a static ideal. To return to the role of craft, the kind of craft futurism that Ngọc, Hân, Tom, and Linh demonstrate in their work speaks to the idea of sustainability as a work in progress and can only be understood through attention to cultural specificity and local conditions. The project's mentoring and exchange ultimately supported these sustainability experiments by facilitating cultural mobility and knowledge exchange.

Finally, the book has provided a space in which to reflect critically and reflexively on processes of cross-cultural exchange, responding to the idea of "cultural complexity" (Ang 2011). Beyond the hope of "decolonizing" knowledge, we have explored the messy and complex practicalities of challenging dominant knowledge systems through cross-cultural exchange—including navigating institutional demands. There is a nuanced "sociality" involved in decolonizing practices, as we have shown, and a need not only to navigate our own implicit and explicit biases, power dynamics, and entrenched ways of thinking, but also to think about the benefits and possibly negative outcomes of research to those involved (Khan 2023). In terms of future directions for the research, there is clearly a need for more work that addresses these practical dimensions of cross-cultural and intercultural exchange. There is also opportunity to deepen knowledge of craft cultures and industries in the Asia Pacific region, including and beyond Vietnam and Australia. In terms of the *đây/đó (here/there)* project, future research avenues include international residencies in both Vietnam and Australia and further in-person collaborations, such as exhibitions and shared workshops, to expand the digital boundaries from the point at which the project began.

The title of the book and project, *đây/đó (here/there)*, points to the role of cultural mobility and intercultural exchange in traversing different worlds and to the importance of finding these spaces for encounter and exchange. It was in the space between "here" and "there" that the learnings of the project occurred. What emerged were the shared goals of creatives in Australia and Vietnam to strive for more equitable, sustainable, and craft-oriented practices across different contexts and conditions in the creative industries and cultural sectors of both places. As mentor Dewi Cooke stated, "Being 'there' or 'here' depends on our subjective perspective, which means that it is completely possible to be flexible. So I think no matter where we are, we can share and cooperate with each other, if we want to" (Hai 2021).

References

Ang, Ien. 2011. "Navigating Complexity: From Cultural Critique to Cultural Intelligence." *Continuum* 25 (6): 779–94.

Hai, A. 2021. "Storytelling 'here/there': Sustainability Comes from Community Connection and Local Quintessence." Vietnam Festival of Creativity & Design 2021. Accessed December 3, 2023. https://vfcd.events/tin-tuc/truyen-ke-day-do/?fbclid=IwAR2fLH1L4tj-ded1BRo9ZNZi6zyxP22TRjOTC2PrZUTDNu-a9Ua-MMYX56VsO.

Khan, R. 2023. "The Sociality of Decolonisation: Making Fashion, Heritage, and Cultural Sustainability in Vietnam." In *Fashion's Transnational Inequalities: Socio-Political, Economic, and Environmental*, edited by A. M. Almila and S. Delice. Routledge.

Notes

1 Ho Chi Minh City is also referred to as Saigon. Saigon was renamed Ho Chi Minh City in 1975, after the Vietnam War (1955–1975), to honor Ho Chi Minh (1890–1969), the former prime minister and revolutionary leader of the Communist Party. Today, both names are used interchangeably.

2 "Naarm" is the Woi Wurrung language name for Melbourne, Australia. It means "place" in the language of the people of the Eastern Kulin nations, the traditional owners of the region.

3 Hemp fabric is made locally by H'mong and Dao women.

4 Confucianism was introduced gradually to Vietnam from China as early as 111 BCE, when Vietnam was under the Chinese Empire (111 BCE–938 CE). This context highlights the many cross-cultural influences that have become embedded in contemporary Vietnamese culture over many generations.

www.ingramcontent.com/pod-product-compliance
Lightning Source LLC
LaVergne TN
LVHW052358100826
845147LV00013B/872

* 9 7 8 1 9 5 6 3 1 3 3 2 1 *